KINGSFORD®

and More
Simple 1-2-3™

Publications International, Ltd.

Favorite Brand Name Recipes at www.fbnr.com

Louis Weber, CEO
Publications International, Ltd.
7373 North Cicero Avenue
Lincolnwood, IL 60712

Pictured on the back cover *(clockwise from top)*: Western Lamb Rib *(page 84)*, Pork and Plum Kabobs *(page 104),* and Glazed Cornish Hens *(page 44).*

ISBN-13: 978-1-4127-2626-9
ISBN-10: 1-4127-2626-3

Manufactured in China.

8 7 6 5 4 3 2 1

Contents

Introduction 4

Starters & Sides 8

Beef 24

Chicken & Turkey 44

Fish & Seafood 64

Lamb 84

Pork 104

Sandwiches & Burgers 124

Salads 144

Index 156

Air Vents: To control temperatures, you'll need to open and close vents to adjust the oxygen supply. There should be vents both underneath the charcoal chamber and in the lid.

Ash Catcher: Most charcoal grills have a device that sweeps used ashes into a disposal pan. It often works by sliding the vent lever back and forth to knock the ashes through the vent holes in the bottom. It helps if the disposal pan can be removed to dump the cooled ashes.

Hinged Grid/Grate: A handy feature that allows you to lift the grid and add more coals or wood to the fire without removing the food. It's especially helpful

Cooking Outdoors

With Kingsford® Charcoal

What is it about grilling that so captures the American imagination?

Is it cooking in the wide open spaces and the great outdoors? Or is it the primitive delight of playing with fire? Maybe it's just how good food tastes when it's kissed with smoke and seared to perfection.

Holding meat on a stick over a fire is certainly among the first cooking methods devised by humans. We've come a long way since then with our fancy grills, custom-made utensils, national barbecue contests, and vehement opinions on the subject. Still, the basics haven't changed. The chemistry of food over fire is a simple and delicious one. Grilling really is one of the easiest and quickest ways to make natural flavors shine. From a toasted marshmallow to a slightly charred T-bone steak, everything from the grill just plain tastes better.

The next few pages go over grilling basics. For those just getting started, there's help choosing the right grill and taking care of it once you get it home. This book also contains recipes sure to tempt you to charge up the grill for parties and quick weeknight dinners alike. It won't be long before you're adding grill marks to everything from tuna to tomatoes. So come outside and light that fire. Grilling will make other kinds of cooking seem tame.

Choosing a Charcoal Grill

Overall Construction: A sturdy, long-lasting grill is heavy and made of high-grade steel rather than aluminum. The finish should be baked-on porcelain-enamel, not just sprayed-on paint. Legs should be welded on. Wheels should be heavy-duty.

Brand Name: Buying a familiar brand name with a reputation for quality is a good bet. Check the warranty period to see if the manufacturer stands behind the product. If you're going to keep a grill for many seasons, replacing grids and other parts will be easier if they're stocked at your local hardware store.

Cooking Grids (Grates): Look for grids made of nickel plated or porcelain-coated cast iron for maximum heat retention, ease of cleaning, and rust resistance. Uncoated stainless steel grids resist rust but may allow food to stick. Uncoated cast iron grids retain heat well, but will require frequent seasoning.

Capacity: Bigger isn't always better. If you'll only be cooking for 2, you don't want to waste charcoal heating up a giant grill whenever you crave a burger. Consider clearance when the grill is covered, too. Whatever you plan to grill should fit comfortably under the grill cover. Also, measure the area where you're planning to place the grill in your backyard. There should be enough room to keep it away from your deck, house, and shrubs.

Taking Care of Your Grill

Your brand new grill will be shiny and pristine, but it won't stay that way. One of the most important steps in caring for any grill is to read and keep the owner's manual, which will give specific dos and don'ts to keep your investment in good condition.

Cleaning the Cooking Surface: Clean the grid each time you grill so food doesn't stick or pick up flavors from your last cooking session. You won't need abrasives or oven cleaners if you take a few minutes for maintenance every time before and after you grill. After the grill is preheated and before you cook, rub the grid with a dry, stiff wire brush. You'll need a long-handled one or an oven mitt to protect yourself. The heat not only sterilizes the grid but makes it easier to get off those last few burned-on bits. When you're through grilling, let the heat do the hard part of the work once again. Then brush the grid thoroughly with the same stiff wire brush.

Keep Your Grill Grid Lubricated: This will help keep it clean. Oil the grid with cooking oil every time you use it. Use a paper towel or clean rag soaked in cooking oil or a can of spray oil. For best results (and good grill marks), oil the grid when it's

if you'll be doing a lot of long, slow barbecuing.

Optional Goodies: Side tables, utensil holders and rotisserie attachments. Some manufacturers are now creating grills with built-in chimney charcoal starters.

Side Baskets: This feature makes it easy to cook over indirect heat because it holds the coals on each side of the grill, making it simple to place a drip pan in the center. If a grill doesn't come with side baskets, you can often buy them to add on later.

Thermometer: It's convenient to have a thermometer that registers the temperature inside a grill that can be read from outside. Opening a grill to check the temperature lowers it drastically and adds to cooking times.

Flare-Ups and How to Handle Them

The bugaboo of every griller, flare-ups happen when grease drips onto hot coals. Flames licking around your food may be exciting to watch, but a charred, blackened surface definitely does not improve flavor. Almost every serious griller has his or her own favorite way of taking care of a flare-up.

Spray Bottle of Water: A spray of water will usually quell the flames in a charcoal grill—temporarily. The trouble is, it won't eliminate the grease, so chances are it will flare up again. Of course, if you continue to spray on water, you'll eventually extinguish the fire.

hot. If you're using cooking spray, remove the grid from the fire wearing a heavy duty grill glove and hold it a safe distance from the grill before spraying.

Caring for the Firebox: Remove cold ashes from the bottom of a charcoal grill. (A garden trowel is a good tool to use to shovel them out.) This makes it easier to build a new fire next time and helps prevent rusting since ashes absorb moisture.

Cleaning Up After Yourself: When you have finished grilling, take a few minutes to put things in order before you put them away. Take the time to gently brush the grid clean of any large clumps of food the may be stuck to it. Open the lower vents so your charcoal burns out completely, but close any vents in your grill's lid to reduce the hazard of debris landing in the grill. Never leave your grill unattended until the fire has completely burned out.

Lighting Your Fire

In the early days of grilling, the height of the flames leaping out of your grill when you lit it was a point of pride. But today we all know that using too much chemical-based lighter fluid can leave a residue that lingers unpleasantly in the flavor of the cooked food. Fortunately, these days there are better lighter fluids and plenty of other options. However you start your fire, first make sure the vents in the bottom of your grill are open so the fire gets needed oxygen.

Lighter Fluid: If you use lighter fluid, read and follow the instructions on the package. Pile the coals in a pyramid, soak them with fluid and the light with a long-handled match or wand-type lighter. NEVER try to add lighter fluid to coals that are already burning. The fire can climb the stream of lighter fluid back toward the can with disastrous results.

Chimney Starter: This hollow metal cylinder allows you to light charcoal quickly and evenly without a drop of lighter fluid. Place the chimney starter on the charcoal grate (not the cooking grid) and put crumpled newspaper in the bottom section. Fill the top section with charcoal (or hardwood). Light the newspaper underneath to ignite the coals and wait until they glow orange red. This process takes 15 to 25 minutes. Wearing a heavy oven mitt to protect your hand, pick up the starter by the handle, dump the coals into the grill, and you're ready to go.

Electric Starter: This device is a looped heating element on a handle. Snuggle it in among the coals and plug it in. It will glow red and ignite the coals. Wait 10 to 15 minutes until most of the coals are lit before removing the starter. Unplug the starter and stow it away from flammable objects. Do not return it to storage until it has cooled completely.

Non-toxic, Paraffin and Sawdust Starters: These cubes, sticks, or blocks can aid in lighting charcoal and can also be used with a chimney starter instead of newspaper. Paraffin starters look like wax ice cubes. Sawdust starters are similar to pressed logs used in fireplaces, but come in sticks that are about five inches long.

Taming the Flames

Anyone who has been served grilled chicken that's burnt black outside, but still raw inside knows that there's more to grilling than building a fire. You need to control the heat and understand the cooking process that's right for the food you want to grill.

Direct Versus Indirect Grilling: There's probably more confusion about these two expressions than any other part of the grilling vocabulary. In the simplest terms, direct grilling is cooking over the heat source. Indirect means what it sounds like it: cooking in heat, but not right over a fire. Direct grilling is perfect for burgers, brats, steaks, and kebabs. Indirect grilling is for food that takes more than 30 minutes to cook, such as a whole chicken, pork shoulder, or leg of lamb. It's always done in a covered grill.

Direct Grilling: To make a direct fire for charcoal grilling, spread the lit coals around with a long-handled implement. You want an even layer of coals, but you may want to leave an area to one side free of charcoal. This will give you a place to move food that is cooking too quickly or that is causing a flare-up.

Indirect Grilling: Arrange the coals in two piles on the sides of the firebox, leaving a space in the center. A drip pan (a disposable aluminum pan) is placed in the center space to collect the fat. The food goes on the grid over the drip pan. In order to keep the fire going, you'll need to replenish the coals at regular intervals. If you add briquets directly to the existing fire, leave the cover off the grill until they catch.

Move the Food: It's much better to move the food to a part of the grid where it's not directly over the fire. That way the fat can burn off the grid without hurting the food. You can achieve this by leaving a fire-free zone when you build your fire, or by moving food to a warming rack. If necessary, you can even take food off the grill for a few moments until the grease on the grid burns off.

Prevention: If you trim meat of unnecessary fat before grilling and go easy on the oil in the marinade, there's less chance of a flare-up. It also helps to drain off most of the marinade before placing food on the grid. If you're experiencing a lot of flare-ups you should thoroughly clean your grill.

Starters & Sides

Italian Grilled Vegetables

4 medium unpeeled red
    potatoes
2 tablespoons orange juice
1 tablespoon balsamic
    vinegar
1 clove garlic, minced
½ teaspoon salt
¼ teaspoon black pepper
⅓ cup plus 3 tablespoons
    olive oil, divided
8 thin slices (4×2 inches)
    ham or prosciutto
3 ounces garlic-flavored
    soft goat cheese, cut
    into 8 pieces
8 asparagus spears
1 (each) red and yellow
    bell peppers, cut in
    half and stem and
    seeds removed
2 small zucchini, cut
    lengthwise into thin
    slices
1 Japanese eggplant, cut
    lengthwise into ¼-inch
    slices
12 large mushrooms
2 poblano peppers, cut
    in half and stems
    and seeds
    removed

1. Prepare grill for direct grilling. Cook potatoes in boiling water until tender. Drain; cool slightly. Cut potatoes into thick slices. Meanwhile, combine juice, vinegar, garlic, salt and black pepper in small bowl; whisk in ⅓ cup oil. Set aside.

2. Wrap each ham slice around 1 piece cheese and 1 asparagus spear. Thread cheese bundles onto wooden skewers. (Soak wooden skewers and picks in hot water 30 minutes to prevent burning.) Brush bundles with remaining 3 tablespoons oil.

3. Grill bell peppers, skin sides down, over medium heat 8 minutes or until skins are charred. Place in large resealable food storage bag; seal. Let stand 5 minutes; discard skins. Grill remaining vegetables on covered grill over medium heat 2 to 5 minutes on each side or until tender. Grill cheese bundles over medium heat until lightly browned. Arrange vegetables and cheese bundles in large glass dish; drizzle with juice mixture, turning to coat. Let stand 15 minutes.

Makes 8 servings

Grilled Cajun Potato Wedges

3 large unpeeled russet
    potatoes, washed
    and scrubbed (about
    2¼ pounds)
¼ cup olive oil
2 cloves garlic, minced
1 teaspoon salt
1 teaspoon paprika
½ teaspoon dried thyme
½ teaspoon dried oregano
¼ teaspoon black pepper
⅛ to ¼ teaspoon ground
    red pepper
2 cups mesquite chips

Makes 4 to 6 servings

1. Preheat oven to 425°F.

2. Cut potatoes in half lengthwise; then cut each half lengthwise into 4 wedges. Place potatoes in large bowl. Add oil and garlic; toss to coat well.

3. Combine salt, paprika, thyme, oregano, black pepper and ground red pepper in small bowl. Sprinkle over potatoes; toss to coat well. Place potato wedges in single layer in shallow roasting pan. (Reserve remaining oil mixture left in large bowl.) Bake 20 minutes.

4. Meanwhile, prepare grill for direct cooking and cover mesquite chips with cold water; soak 20 minutes. Drain mesquite chips; sprinkle over coals. Place potato wedges on their sides on grid. Grill potato wedges, on covered grill, over medium coals 15 to 20 minutes or until potatoes are browned and fork-tender, brushing with reserved oil mixture halfway through grilling time and turning once with tongs.

Starters & Sides

Herbed Mushroom Vegetable Medley

Makes 4 servings

4 ounces button or crimini mushrooms
1 medium red or yellow bell pepper, cut into ¼-inch-wide strips
1 medium zucchini, cut crosswise into ¼-inch-thick slices
1 medium yellow squash, cut crosswise into ¼-inch-thick slices
3 tablespoons butter or margarine, melted
1 tablespoon chopped fresh thyme *or* 1 teaspoon dried thyme
1 tablespoon chopped fresh basil *or* 1 teaspoon dried basil
1 tablespoon chopped fresh chives or green onion tops
1 clove garlic, minced
¼ teaspoon salt
¼ teaspoon black pepper

1. Prepare grill for direct cooking.

2. Cut thin slice from base of mushroom stems with paring knife; discard. Thinly slice mushroom stems and caps. Combine mushrooms, bell pepper, zucchini and squash in large bowl. Combine butter, thyme, basil, chives, garlic, salt and black pepper in small bowl. Pour over vegetable mixture; toss to coat well.

3. Transfer mixture to 20×14-inch sheet of heavy-duty foil; wrap. Place foil packet on grid. Grill packet on covered grill over medium coals 20 to 25 minutes or until vegetables are fork-tender. Open packet carefully to serve.

Starters & Sides

Portobello Mushrooms Sesame

4 large portobello
   mushrooms
2 tablespoons sweet rice
   wine
2 tablespoons
   reduced-sodium
   soy sauce
2 cloves garlic, minced
1 teaspoon dark sesame
   oil

Makes 4 servings

1. Prepare grill for direct grilling.

2. Remove and discard stems from mushrooms; set caps aside. Combine remaining ingredients in small bowl.

3. Brush both sides of mushroom caps with soy sauce mixture. Grill mushrooms, top sides up, on covered grill over medium coals 3 to 4 minutes. Brush tops with soy sauce mixture; turn over. Grill 2 minutes more or until mushrooms are lightly browned. Turn again; grill, basting frequently, 4 to 5 minutes or until tender when pressed with back of metal spatula. Remove mushrooms; cut diagonally into ½-inch-thick slices.

6 ears fresh corn
¼ cup margarine or butter, melted
1 tablespoon chopped fresh parsley
2 teaspoons prepared horseradish
¼ teaspoon paprika
¼ teaspoon black pepper
⅛ teaspoon salt

Zesty Corn-on-the-Cob

Makes 6 servings

1. Pull outer husks from top to base of each corn ear; leave husks attached to ear. Strip away silk. Trim any blemishes from corn. Place corn in large bowl. Cover with cold water; soak 20 to 30 minutes.

2. Prepare grill for direct cooking. Remove corn from water; pat kernels dry with paper towels. Combine margarine, parsley, horseradish, paprika, pepper and salt in small bowl. Spread about half of margarine mixture evenly over kernels. Bring husks back up each ear of corn; secure at top with wet string.

3. Place corn on grid. Grill, covered, over medium-high heat 15 to 20 minutes or until corn is hot and tender, turning every 5 minutes. Transfer corn to serving plate. Remove front half of husks on each piece of corn; brush with remaining margarine mixture.

Starters & Sides

Roasted Eggplant Dip

2 eggplants (about
    1 pound each)
¼ cup lemon juice
3 tablespoons sesame
    tahini*
4 cloves garlic, minced
2 teaspoons hot pepper
    sauce
½ teaspoon salt
   Paprika
1 tablespoon chopped
    fresh parsley
   Red chili pepper slices**
    (optional)
   Pita bread rounds, cut
    into wedges

*Available in the ethnic section of the supermarket or in Middle Eastern grocery stores.

**Jalapeño peppers can sting and irritate the skin, so wear rubber gloves when handling peppers and do not touch your eyes.

Makes 8 (¼-cup) servings

1. Prepare grill for direct cooking. Prick eggplants in several places with fork. Place eggplants on grid. Grill, covered, over medium-high heat 30 to 40 minutes or until skin is black and blistered and pulp is soft, turning often. Peel eggplants when cool enough to handle. Let cool to room temperature.

2. Place eggplant pulp in food processor with lemon juice, tahini, garlic, pepper sauce and salt; process until smooth. Refrigerate at least 1 hour before serving to allow flavors to blend. Sprinkle top with paprika and parsley and red pepper slices; serve with pita bread.

Starters & Sides

¾ **cup fresh orange juice**
⅓ **cup fresh lime juice**
2 **tablespoons tequila**
2 **jalapeño peppers,***
   seeded and minced
2 **tablespoons chopped**
   fresh cilantro, chives
   or green onion tops
1 **teaspoon honey**
1 **teaspoon ground cumin**
1 **teaspoon olive oil**
10 **squid, cleaned and cut**
   into rings and tentacles
½ **pound medium shrimp,**
   peeled, deveined and
   tails removed
2 **lobster tails (8 ounces**
   each), meat removed
   and shells discarded

*Jalapeño peppers can sting and irritate the skin, so wear rubber gloves when handling peppers and do not touch your eyes.

Starters & Sides

Grilled Lobster, Shrimp and Calamari Seviche

Makes 6 appetizer servings

1. To make marinade, combine orange juice, lime juice, tequila, jalapeños, cilantro and honey in medium glass bowl. Measure ¼ cup marinade into small glass bowl; stir in cumin and oil. Set aside. Refrigerate remaining marinade.

2. Bring 1 quart water in 2-quart saucepan to a boil over high heat. Add squid; cook 30 seconds or until opaque. Drain. Rinse under cold water; drain. Add squid to refrigerated marinade. Thread shrimp onto metal skewers. Brush shrimp and lobster with reserved ¼ cup marinade.

3. Prepare grill for direct grilling. Place shrimp on grid. Grill shrimp on uncovered grill, over medium-hot coals, 2 to 3 minutes per side or until shrimp turn pink and opaque. Remove shrimp from skewers; add to squid. Place lobster on grid. Grill 5 minutes per side or until meat turns opaque and is cooked through. Slice lobster meat into ¼-inch-thick slices; add to squid and shrimp mixture. Refrigerate at least 2 hours or overnight.

4 cups chicken broth
1 small onion, minced
4 cloves garlic, minced
1 tablespoon minced fresh rosemary *or* 1 teaspoon dried rosemary
½ teaspoon salt
1¼ cups yellow cornmeal
6 tablespoons grated Parmesan cheese
1 tablespoon olive oil, divided

Parmesan Polenta

Makes 6 servings

1. Spray 11×7-inch baking pan with nonstick cooking spray; set aside. Spray one side of 7-inch-long sheet of waxed paper with cooking spray; set aside. Combine chicken broth, onion, garlic, rosemary and salt in medium saucepan. Bring to a boil over high heat; add cornmeal gradually, stirring constantly. Reduce heat to medium and simmer 30 minutes or until mixture has consistency of thick mashed potatoes. Remove from heat and stir in cheese.

2. Spread polenta evenly in prepared pan; place waxed paper, sprayed-side down, on polenta and smooth. (If surface is bumpy, it is more likely to stick to grill.) Cool on wire rack 15 minutes or until firm. Remove waxed paper; cut into 6 squares. Remove squares from pan.

3. To prevent sticking, spray grid with cooking spray. Prepare coals for grilling. Brush tops of squares with half the oil. Grill oil-side down on covered grill over medium to low coals for 6 to 8 minutes or until golden. Brush with remaining oil and gently turn over. Grill 6 to 8 minutes more or until golden. Serve warm.

Starters & Sides

Beef

Ginger Beef and Carrot Kabobs

¾ pound boneless beef top sirloin steak (1 inch thick), cut into 1-inch cubes
¼ cup reduced-sodium soy sauce
1 tablespoon water
1 tablespoon honey
1 teaspoon olive oil
¼ teaspoon ground ginger
¼ teaspoon ground allspice
⅛ teaspoon ground red pepper
1 clove garlic, minced
2 medium carrots, cut into 1-inch pieces (1½ cups)
4 green onions, trimmed to 4-inch pieces

1. Place beef in large resealable food storage bag. Combine soy sauce, water, honey, oil, ginger, allspice, red pepper and garlic in small bowl. Pour over meat in bag. Seal bag; turn to coat meat. Marinate in refrigerator 4 to 16 hours, turning bag occasionally.

2. Meanwhile, place 1 inch water in medium saucepan. Bring water to a boil. Add carrots. Cover; cook 5 minutes or until crisp-tender. Drain.

3. Prepare grill for direct cooking. Drain meat. Discard marinade. Alternately thread meat and carrot pieces onto 4 soaked wooden skewers. Add green onion piece to end of each skewer.

4. Grill kabobs over medium coals 11 to 14 minutes or until meat is tender, turning once during grilling.

Makes 4 servings

Jamaican Steak

2 pounds beef flank steak
¼ cup packed brown sugar
3 tablespoons orange juice
3 tablespoons lime juice
3 cloves garlic, minced
1 piece (1½×1 inch) fresh
    ginger, minced
2 teaspoons grated
    orange peel
2 teaspoons grated lime
    peel
1 teaspoon salt
1 teaspoon black pepper
¼ teaspoon ground
    cinnamon
⅛ teaspoon ground cloves
    Shredded orange peel
    Shredded lime peel

Makes 6 servings

Score both sides of beef.* Combine sugar, juices, garlic, ginger, grated peels, salt, pepper, cinnamon and cloves in 2-quart glass dish. Add beef; turn to coat. Cover and refrigerate steak at least 2 hours. Remove beef from marinade; discard marinade. Grill beef over medium-hot KINGSFORD® Briquets about 6 minutes per side until medium-rare or to desired doneness. Garnish with shredded orange and lime peels.

To score flank steak, cut ¼-inch-deep diagonal lines about 1 inch apart in surface of steak to form diamond-shaped design.

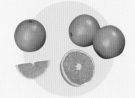

Teriyaki Glazed Beef Kabobs

1¼ to 1½ pounds beef top or bottom sirloin, cut into 1-inch cubes
½ cup bottled teriyaki sauce
1 teaspoon Oriental sesame oil (optional)
1 clove garlic, minced
8 to 12 green onions
1 or 2 plum tomatoes, cut into slices (optional)

Makes 4 servings

Thread beef cubes onto metal or bamboo skewers. (Soak bamboo skewers in water for at least 20 minutes to keep them from burning.) Combine teriyaki sauce, sesame oil, if desired, and garlic in small bowl. Brush beef and onions with part of glaze, saving some for grilling; let beef stand 15 to 30 minutes.

Oil hot grid to help prevent sticking. Grill beef, on covered grill, over medium KINGSFORD® Briquets, 6 to 9 minutes for medium doneness, turning several times and brushing with glaze. Add onions and tomatoes, if desired, to grid 3 to 4 minutes after beef; grill until onions and tomatoes are tender. Remove from grill; brush skewers, onions and tomatoes with remaining glaze.

1 tablespoon paprika
2 teaspoons salt
1 teaspoon black pepper
¼ teaspoon ground red
    pepper
1 small beef brisket,
    trimmed (about
    1¼ pounds)
Texas BBQ Sauce
    (recipe follows)

Texas BBQ Sauce

1½ cups ketchup
¾ cup honey
½ cup cider or white
    vinegar
1 small onion, finely
    chopped
2 tablespoons
    Worcestershire sauce
1 jalapeño pepper,*
    seeded and minced
1 tablespoon mustard
1 teaspoon olive oil

*Jalapeño peppers can sting and
irritate the skin, so wear rubber
gloves when handling peppers
and do not touch your eyes.*

Texas Beef Brisket

Makes 4 servings

1. Combine paprika, salt, black and red pepper in small bowl; mix well. Rub spice mixture onto brisket. Cover; marinate in refrigerator overnight.

2. Prepare Texas BBQ Sauce; set aside. Prepare grill for direct cooking.

3. Place brisket on grid. Grill, covered, over medium heat 2½ hours or until brisket offers a slight resistance when pierced; check occasionally and baste with sauce as needed. Boil any remaining sauce and serve on the side for dipping.

Texas BBQ Sauce: Combine all ingredients in medium bowl; mix well.

Makes about 3 cups

Spicy Smoked Beef Ribs

Makes 4 to 6 servings

Wood chunks or chips for smoking
4 to 6 pounds beef back ribs, cut into 3 to 4 rib pieces
Black pepper
1⅓ cups barbecue sauce, divided
2 teaspoons hot pepper sauce or Szechwan chili sauce
Beer at room temperature or hot tap water

1. Prepare grill for indirect grilling. Soak 4 wood chunks or several handfuls of wood chips in water; drain.

2. Spread ribs on baking sheet or tray; season with pepper. Combine barbecue sauce and hot pepper sauce. Brush ribs with half of sauce. Marinate in the refrigerator 30 minutes to 1 hour.

3. Arrange low coals on each side of rectangular metal or foil drip pan. (Since the ribs have been brushed with sauce before cooking, low heat is needed to keep them moist.) Pour in beer to fill pan half full. Add soaked wood (all the chunks; part of chips) to fire.

4. Oil hot grid to help prevent sticking. Place ribs on grid, meaty side up, directly above drip pan. Cook ribs, on covered grill, about 1 hour, brushing remaining sauce over ribs 2 or 3 times during cooking. If grill has thermometer, maintain cooking temperature between 250°F to 275°F. Add a few more briquets after 30 minutes, or as necessary, to maintain constant temperature. Add more soaked wood chips every 30 minutes, if necessary. Serve with grilled corn-on-the-cob, if desired.

Beef with Dry Spice Rub

3 tablespoons firmly packed brown sugar
1 tablespoon yellow mustard seeds
1 tablespoon whole coriander seeds
1 tablespoon black peppercorns
4 cloves garlic
1½ to 2 pounds beef top round (London Broil) steak, about 1½ inches thick
Vegetable or olive oil
Salt

Makes 6 servings

Place sugar, mustard seeds, coriander seeds, peppercorns and garlic in blender or food processor; process until seeds and garlic are crushed. Rub beef with oil; pat on spice mixture. Season generously with salt.

Lightly oil hot grid to prevent sticking. Grill beef, on covered grill, over medium-low KINGSFORD® Briquets 16 to 20 minutes for medium rare or until desired doneness, turning once. Let stand 5 minutes before cutting across the grain into thin diagonal slices.

Guadalajara Beef and Salsa

1 bottle (12 ounces) Mexican dark beer*
¼ cup soy sauce
2 cloves garlic, minced
1 teaspoon ground cumin
1 teaspoon chili powder
1 teaspoon hot pepper sauce
4 boneless beef sirloin or top loin strip steaks (4 to 6 ounces each)
Salt and black pepper
Red, green and yellow bell peppers, cut lengthwise into quarters, seeded (optional)
Salsa (recipe follows)
Flour tortillas (optional)
Lime wedges

*Substitute any beer for Mexican dark beer.

Salsa

2 cups coarsely chopped seeded tomatoes
2 green onions with tops, sliced
1 clove garlic, minced
1 to 2 teaspoons minced seeded jalapeño or serrano chili pepper,** fresh or canned
1 tablespoon olive or vegetable oil
2 to 3 teaspoons lime juice
8 to 10 sprigs fresh cilantro, minced (optional)
½ teaspoon salt or to taste
½ teaspoon sugar or to taste
¼ teaspoon black pepper

**Jalapeño peppers can sting and irritate the skin; wear rubber gloves when handling and do not touch eyes. Wash hands after handling.

Makes 4 servings

Combine beer, soy sauce, garlic, cumin, chili powder and hot pepper sauce in large shallow glass dish or large heavy plastic food storage bag. Add beef; cover dish or close bag. Marinate in refrigerator up to 12 hours, turning beef several times. Remove beef from marinade; discard marinade. Season with salt and black pepper.

Oil hot grid to help prevent sticking. Grill beef and bell peppers, if desired, on covered grill, over medium KINGSFORD® Briquets, 8 to 12 minutes, turning once. Beef should be of medium doneness and peppers should be tender. Serve with salsa, tortillas, if desired, and lime wedges.

Salsa: Combine tomatoes, green onions, garlic, chili pepper, oil and lime juice in medium bowl. Stir in cilantro, if desired. Season with salt, sugar and black pepper. Adjust seasonings to taste, adding lime juice or chili pepper, if desired.

Makes about 2 cups

Skewered Beef Strips with Spicy Honey Glaze

1 beef top sirloin steak
(about 1 pound)
⅓ cup soy sauce
2 tablespoons white
vinegar
1 teaspoon ground ginger
⅛ teaspoon ground red
pepper
⅓ cup honey

Makes 4 servings

1. Slice beef across the grain into ¼-inch-thick strips. Thread beef strips onto 12 wooden skewers and place in large glass baking dish. (Soak skewers in cold water 20 minutes before using to prevent them from burning.)

2. Prepare grill for direct cooking. Combine soy sauce, vinegar, ginger and red pepper; pour over skewers and marinate 10 minutes, turning once.

3. Drain marinade into small saucepan; stir in honey and brush mixture over beef. Bring remaining mixture to a boil; boil 2 minutes.

4. Grill skewered beef 3 to 4 minutes. Serve remaining honey glaze as dipping sauce.

Vietnamese Loin Steaks with Black Bean Relish

Makes 4 servings

1 stalk lemongrass, outer leaves and tough upper stalk removed
1 tablespoon sugar
1 tablespoon fish sauce
1 teaspoon minced garlic
½ to 1 teaspoon hot chili oil
2 boneless beef top loin (strip) steaks (8 ounces each)
1 can (about 8¾ ounces) whole baby corn (about 8 cobs), rinsed and drained
1 can (about 15 ounces) black beans, rinsed and drained
1 cup diced mango
½ green bell pepper, cut into strips
2 tablespoons chopped red onion
1 jalapeño pepper,* seeded and sliced (optional)
Juice of ½ lemon
½ teaspoon vegetable oil
½ teaspoon honey
⅛ teaspoon salt

Jalapeño peppers can sting and irritate the skin, so wear rubber gloves when handling peppers and do not touch your eyes.

1. Flatten lemongrass with meat mallet and mince. Combine with sugar, fish sauce, garlic and chili oil in baking dish. Cut each steak lengthwise into 2 strips. Place in dish with marinade, coating both sides. Cover; refrigerate 1 hour, turning once.

2. Halve corn cobs diagonally; combine with beans, mango, bell pepper, onion and jalapeño, if desired, in large bowl. Combine lemon juice, oil, honey and salt in small bowl; stir into bean mixture.

3. Grill steaks over medium heat, uncovered, 10 to 12 minutes for medium-rare to medium or until desired doneness, turning once. Serve with relish.

Rosemary Steak

4 boneless beef top loin (New York strip) steaks (about 6 ounces each)

2 tablespoons minced fresh rosemary

2 cloves garlic, minced

1 tablespoon extra-virgin olive oil

1 teaspoon grated lemon peel

1 teaspoon coarsely ground black pepper

½ teaspoon salt
Fresh rosemary sprigs

Makes 4 servings

Score steaks in diamond pattern on both sides. Combine minced rosemary, garlic, oil, lemon peel, pepper and salt in small bowl; rub mixture onto surface of meat. Cover and refrigerate at least 15 minutes. Grill steaks over medium-hot KINGSFORD® Briquets about 4 minutes per side until medium-rare or to desired doneness. Cut steaks diagonally into ½-inch-thick slices. Garnish with rosemary sprigs.

Glazed Cornish Hens

2 fresh or thawed frozen Cornish game hens (1½ pounds each)
3 tablespoons fresh lemon juice
1 clove garlic, minced
¼ cup orange marmalade
1 tablespoon coarse-grain or country-style mustard
2 teaspoons grated fresh ginger

1. Remove giblets from cavities of hens; reserve for another use. Split hens in half on cutting board with sharp knife or poultry shears, cutting through breastbones and backbones. Rinse hens with cold water; pat dry with paper towels. Place hen halves in large resealable food storage bag.

2. Combine juice and garlic in small bowl; pour over hens in bag. Seal bag tightly, turning to coat. Marinate in refrigerator 30 minutes.

3. Meanwhile, prepare grill for direct grilling over medium-hot heat.

4. Drain hens; discard marinade. Place hens, skin sides up, on grid. Grill hens, on covered grill, over medium-hot coals 20 minutes.

5. Meanwhile, combine marmalade, mustard and ginger in small bowl. Brush one-half of marmalade mixture evenly over hens. Grill, covered, 10 minutes. Brush with remaining mixture. Grill, covered, 5 to 10 minutes more until fork can be inserted into hens with ease and juices run clear, not pink. Serve immediately.

Makes 4 servings

Herb Garlic Grilled Chicken

Makes 4 servings

¼ cup chopped fresh
parsley
1½ tablespoons minced
garlic
4 teaspoons grated lemon
peel
1 tablespoon chopped
fresh mint
1 chicken (2½ to
3 pounds), quartered

Combine parsley, garlic, lemon peel and mint. Loosen skin from breast and thigh portions of chicken quarters by running fingers between skin and meat. Rub some of seasoning mixture evenly over meat under skin, replace skin and rub remaining seasonings over outside of chicken to cover evenly. Arrange medium-hot KINGSFORD® Briquets on one side of covered grill. Place chicken on grid opposite coals. Cover grill and cook chicken 45 to 55 minutes, turning once or twice. Chicken is done when juices run clear.

Chicken & Turkey

Mediterranean Chicken Kabobs

Makes 8 servings

2 pounds boneless skinless chicken breasts or chicken tenders, cut into 1-inch pieces

1 small eggplant, peeled and cut into 1-inch pieces

1 medium zucchini, cut crosswise into ½-inch slices

2 medium onions, each cut into 8 wedges

16 medium mushrooms, stems removed

16 cherry tomatoes

1 cup fat-free reduced-sodium chicken broth

⅔ cup balsamic vinegar

3 tablespoons olive oil

2 tablespoons dried mint

4 teaspoons dried basil

1 tablespoon dried oregano

2 teaspoons grated lemon peel

Chopped fresh parsley (optional)

4 cups hot cooked couscous

1. Alternately thread chicken, eggplant, zucchini, onions, mushrooms and tomatoes onto 16 metal skewers; place in large glass baking dish.

2. Combine chicken broth, vinegar, oil, mint, basil and oregano in small bowl; pour over kabobs. Cover; marinate in refrigerator 2 hours, turning kabobs occasionally. Remove kabobs from marinade; discard marinade.

3. Prepare grill for direct cooking; spray grid with nonstick cooking spray. Preheat grill to medium hot. Grill the kabobs on a covered grill over medium-hot coals 10 to 15 minutes or until chicken is no longer pink in center. Turn kabobs halfway through cooking time.

4. Stir lemon peel and parsley into couscous; serve with kabobs.

Chicken & Turkey

Classic Grilled Chicken

Makes 6 servings

1 whole frying chicken*
(3½ pounds),
quartered
¼ cup lemon juice
¼ cup olive oil
2 tablespoons soy sauce
2 large cloves garlic,
minced
½ teaspoon sugar
½ teaspoon ground cumin
¼ teaspoon black pepper

*Substitute 3½ pounds chicken parts for whole chicken, if desired. Grill legs and thighs about 35 minutes and breast halves about 25 minutes or until chicken is no longer pink in center, turning once.

Rinse chicken under cold running water; pat dry with paper towels. Arrange chicken in 13×9×2-inch glass baking dish. Combine remaining ingredients in small bowl; pour half of mixture over chicken. Cover and refrigerate chicken at least 1 hour or overnight. Cover and reserve remaining mixture in refrigerator to use for basting. Remove chicken from marinade; discard marinade. Arrange medium KINGSFORD® Briquets on each side of large rectangular metal or foil drip pan. Pour hot tap water into drip pan until half full. Place chicken on grid directly above drip pan. Grill chicken, skin side down, on covered grill 25 minutes. Baste with reserved mixture. Turn chicken; cook 20 to 25 minutes or until juices run clear and chicken is no longer pink in center.

Chicken & Turkey

2 tablespoons olive oil
1 clove garlic, pressed
1 teaspoon ground cumin
1 teaspoon chili powder
**1 teaspoon dried oregano
  leaves**
½ teaspoon salt
**1 pound skinless boneless
  chicken breast halves
  or thighs**

Southwest Chicken

Makes 8 servings

Combine oil, garlic, cumin, chili powder, oregano and salt; brush over both sides of chicken to coat. Grill chicken over medium-hot KINGSFORD® Briquets 8 to 10 minutes or until chicken is no longer pink, turning once. Serve immediately or use in Build a Burrito, Taco Salad or other favorite recipes.

Note: Southwest Chicken can be grilled ahead and refrigerated for several days or frozen for longer storage.

Build a Burrito: Top warm large flour tortillas with strips of Southwest Chicken and your choice of drained canned black beans, cooked brown or white rice, shredded cheese, salsa verde, shredded lettuce, sliced black olives and chopped cilantro. Fold in sides and roll to enclose filling. Heat in microwave oven at HIGH until heated through. (Or, wrap in foil and heat in preheated 350°F oven.)

Taco Salad: For a quick one-dish meal, layer strips of Southwest Chicken with tomato wedges, blue or traditional corn tortilla chips, sliced black olives, shredded romaine or iceberg lettuce, shredded cheese and avocado slices. Serve with salsa, sour cream, guacamole or a favorite dressing.

Thai Barbecued Chicken

1 cup coarsely chopped
  fresh cilantro
2 jalapeño peppers,*
  coarsely chopped
8 cloves garlic, peeled and
  coarsely chopped
2 tablespoons fish sauce
1 tablespoon packed
  brown sugar
1 teaspoon curry powder
  Grated peel of 1 lemon
3 pounds chicken pieces

Jalapeño peppers can sting and irritate the skin, so wear rubber gloves when handling peppers and do not touch your eyes.

Makes 4 servings

1. Place cilantro, jalapeño peppers, garlic, fish sauce, brown sugar, curry powder and lemon peel in blender or food processor; blend to form coarse paste.

2. Work fingers between skin and meat on breast and thigh pieces. Rub about 1 teaspoon seasoning paste under skin on each piece. Rub chicken pieces on all sides with remaining paste. Place chicken in large resealable food storage bag or covered container; marinate in refrigerator 3 to 4 hours or overnight.

3. Prepare grill for direct cooking.** Brush grid lightly with oil. Grill chicken over medium coals, skin side down, about 10 minutes or until well browned. Turn chicken and grill 20 to 30 minutes more or until chicken is cooked through (170°F for breast meat; 180°F for dark meat). Thighs and legs may require 10 to 15 minutes more cooking time than breasts. If chicken is browned on both sides but still needs additional cooking, move to edge of grill, away from direct heat, to finish cooking.

**To cook in oven, place chicken skin side up in lightly oiled baking pan. Bake in preheated 375°F oven 30 to 45 minutes or until no longer pink in center.

Lemon Herbed Chicken

½ cup butter or margarine
½ cup vegetable oil
⅓ cup lemon juice
2 tablespoons finely chopped parsley
2 tablespoons garlic salt
1 teaspoon dried rosemary, crushed
1 teaspoon dried summer savory, crushed
½ teaspoon dried thyme, crushed
¼ teaspoon coarsely cracked black pepper
6 chicken quarters (breast-wing or thigh-drumstick combinations)

Makes 6 servings

Combine butter, oil, lemon juice, parsley, garlic salt, rosemary, summer savory, thyme and pepper in small saucepan. Heat until butter melts. Place chicken in shallow glass dish. Brush with some of sauce. Let stand 10 to 15 minutes.

Oil hot grid to help prevent sticking. Place dark meat pieces on grill 10 minutes before white meat pieces (dark meat takes longer to cook). Grill chicken, on uncovered grill, over medium-hot KINGSFORD® Briquets, 30 to 45 minutes for breast quarters or 50 to 60 minutes for leg quarters. Chicken is done when meat is no longer pink by bone. Turn quarters over and baste with sauce every 10 minutes.

Chicken Ribbons Satay

½ cup creamy peanut
   butter
½ cup water
¼ cup soy sauce
4 cloves garlic, sliced
3 tablespoons lemon juice
2 tablespoons packed
   brown sugar
¾ teaspoon ground ginger
½ teaspoon crushed red
   pepper flakes
4 boneless skinless chicken
   breast halves
   Sliced green onion tops
   for garnish

Makes 4 servings

Combine peanut butter, water, soy sauce, garlic, lemon juice,
brown sugar, ginger and red pepper flakes in a small saucepan.
Cook over medium heat 1 minute or until smooth; cool. Remove
garlic from sauce; discard. Reserve half of sauce for dipping.
Cut chicken lengthwise into 1-inch-wide strips. Thread onto
8 metal or bamboo skewers. (Soak bamboo skewers in water
at least 20 minutes to keep them from burning.)

Oil hot grid to help prevent sticking. Grill chicken, on a covered
grill, over medium-hot KINGSFORD® Briquets, 6 to 8 minutes until
chicken is no longer pink in center, turning once. Baste with sauce
once or twice during cooking. Serve with reserved sauce garnished
with sliced green onion.

Turkey Teriyaki with Grilled Mushrooms

1¼ pounds turkey breast slices, tenderloins or medallions

¼ cup sake or sherry wine

¼ cup soy sauce

3 tablespoons granulated sugar, brown sugar or honey

1 piece (1-inch cube) fresh ginger, minced

3 cloves garlic, minced

1 tablespoon vegetable oil

½ pound mushrooms

4 green onions, cut into 2-inch pieces

Makes 4 servings

Cut turkey slices into long 2-inch-wide strips.* Combine sake, soy sauce, sugar, ginger, garlic and oil in 2-quart glass dish. Add turkey; turn to coat. Cover and refrigerate 15 minutes or overnight. Remove turkey from marinade; discard marinade. Thread turkey onto metal or wooden skewers, alternating with mushrooms and green onions. (Soak wooden skewers in hot water 30 minutes to prevent burning.) Grill on covered grill over medium-hot KINGSFORD® Briquets about 3 minutes per side until turkey is cooked through.

Do not cut tenderloins or medallions.

1 cup orange juice
¼ cup lemon juice
¼ cup lime juice
2 cloves garlic, pressed or minced
4 boneless skinless chicken breast halves
Salt and black pepper
Citrus Tarragon Butter (recipe follows)
Hot cooked couscous with green onion slices and slivered almonds (optional)
Lemon and lime slices and Italian parsley for garnish

Citrus Tarragon Butter

½ cup butter, softened
1 tablespoon finely chopped fresh tarragon
1 tablespoon lemon juice
1 tablespoon orange juice
1 teaspoon finely grated orange peel
1 teaspoon finely grated lemon peel

Citrus Marinated Chicken

Makes 4 servings

Combine orange, lemon and lime juices and garlic in a shallow glass dish or large heavy plastic bag. Add chicken; cover dish or close bag. Marinate in refrigerator no more than 2 hours. (Lemon and lime juice will "cook" the chicken if it's left in too long.) Remove chicken from marinade; discard marinade. Season chicken with salt and pepper.

Oil hot grid to help prevent sticking. Grill chicken, on a covered grill, over medium KINGSFORD® Briquets, 6 to 8 minutes until chicken is cooked through, turning once. Serve topped with a dollop of Citrus Tarragon Butter. Serve over couscous, if desired. Garnish, if desired.

Citrus Tarragon Butter: Beat butter in a small bowl until soft and light. Stir in remaining ingredients. Cover and refrigerate until ready to serve.

Makes about ½ cup

Fish & Seafood

Grilled Fish with Buttery Lemon Parsley

6 tablespoons margarine or butter
3 tablespoons finely chopped parsley
1 teaspoon grated lemon zest
½ teaspoon salt
½ teaspoon dried rosemary
6 (6 ounces each) fish fillets, such as grouper, snapper or any lean white fish
Nonstick cooking spray
3 medium lemons, halved

1. Preheat grill to medium-high heat. Coat cold grill rack with cooking spray; place over heat.

2. Combine margarine, parsley, lemon zest, salt and rosemary in small bowl; set aside.

3. Coat fish with cooking spray; place on grid. Grill, uncovered, 3 minutes. Turn; grill 2 to 3 minutes longer or until opaque in center.

4. To serve, squeeze juice from 1 lemon half evenly over each fillet. Top with equal amounts of parsley mixture.

Makes 6 servings

Cajun Grilled Shrimp

3 green onions, minced
2 tablespoons lemon juice
3 cloves garlic, minced
2 teaspoons paprika
1 teaspoon salt
¼ to ½ teaspoon black
    pepper
¼ to ½ teaspoon cayenne
    pepper
1 tablespoon olive oil
1½ pounds shrimp, shelled
    with tails intact,
    deveined
Lemon wedges

Makes 4 servings

Combine onions, lemon juice, garlic, paprika, salt and peppers in 2-quart glass dish; stir in oil. Add shrimp; turn to coat. Cover and refrigerate at least 15 minutes. Thread shrimp onto metal or wooden skewers. (Soak wooden skewers in hot water 30 minutes to prevent burning.) Grill shrimp over medium-hot KINGSFORD® Briquets about 2 minutes per side until opaque. Serve immediately with lemon wedges.

Tomato Basil Butter Sauce (recipe follows)
4 fish steaks, such as halibut, swordfish, tuna or salmon (at least ¾ inch thick)
Olive oil
Salt and black pepper
Fresh basil leaves and summer squash slices for garnish
Hot cooked seasoned noodles (optional)

Tomato Basil Butter Sauce

4 tablespoons butter or margarine, softened, divided
1½ cups chopped seeded peeled tomatoes (about 1 pound)
½ teaspoon sugar
1 clove garlic, minced
Salt and black pepper
1½ tablespoons very finely chopped fresh basil

Grilled Fish Steaks with Tomato Basil Butter Sauce

Makes 4 servings

Prepare Tomato Basil Butter Sauce; set aside. Rinse fish; pat dry with paper towels. Brush one side of fish lightly with oil; season with salt and pepper.

Oil hot grid to help prevent sticking. Grill fish, oil side down, on a covered grill, over medium KINGSFORD® Briquets, 6 to 10 minutes. Halfway through cooking time, brush top with oil and season with salt and pepper, then turn and continue grilling until fish turns from translucent to opaque throughout. (Grilling time depends on the thickness of fish; allow 3 to 5 minutes for each ½ inch of thickness.) Serve with Tomato Basil Butter Sauce. Garnish with basil leaves and squash slices. Serve with noodles, if desired.

Tomato Basil Butter Sauce: Melt 1 tablespoon butter in
a small skillet. Add tomatoes, sugar and garlic. Cook over medium-low heat, stirring frequently, until liquid evaporates and mixture thickens. Remove pan from heat; stir in remaining butter until mixture has a saucelike consistency. Season to taste with salt and pepper, then stir in basil.

Makes about 1 cup

Fish & Seafood

Grilled Fish with Orange-Chile Salsa

Makes 4 servings

3 medium oranges, peeled and sectioned* (about 1¼ cups segments)

¼ cup finely diced green, red or yellow bell pepper

3 tablespoons chopped fresh cilantro, divided

3 tablespoons lime juice, divided

1 tablespoon honey

1 teaspoon minced, seeded serrano pepper *or* 1 tablespoon minced jalapeño pepper**

1¼ pounds firm white fish fillets, such as orange roughy, lingcod, halibut or red snapper

Lime slices

Zucchini ribbons, cooked

Canned mandarin orange segments can be substituted for fresh orange segments, if desired.

**Chile peppers can sting and irritate the skin, so wear rubber gloves when handling peppers and do not touch your eyes. Wash hands after handling peppers.*

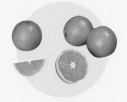

To prepare Orange-Chile Salsa, combine orange segments, bell pepper, 2 tablespoons cilantro, 2 tablespoons lime juice, honey and serrano pepper. Set aside.

Season fish fillets with remaining 1 tablespoon cilantro and 1 tablespoon lime juice. Lightly oil grid to prevent sticking. Grill fish on covered grill over medium KINGSFORD® Briquets 5 minutes. Turn and top with lime slices, if desired. Grill about 5 minutes until fish flakes easily when tested with fork. Serve with Orange-Chile Salsa. Garnish with zucchini ribbons.

Note: Allow about 10 minutes grilling time per inch thickness of fish fillets.

Lobster Tails with Tasty Butters

Hot & Spicy Butter,
Scallion Butter or
Chili-Mustard Butter
(recipes follow)
4 fresh or thawed frozen
lobster tails (about
5 ounces each)

Tasty Butters

Hot & Spicy Butter
⅓ cup butter or margarine,
melted
1 tablespoon chopped
onion
2 to 3 teaspoons hot
pepper sauce
1 teaspoon dried thyme
¼ teaspoon ground allspice

Scallion Butter
⅓ cup butter or margarine,
melted
1 tablespoon finely
chopped green onion
tops
1 tablespoon lemon juice
1 teaspoon grated lemon
peel
¼ teaspoon black pepper

Chili-Mustard Butter
⅓ cup butter or margarine,
melted
1 tablespoon chopped
onion
1 tablespoon Dijon
mustard
1 teaspoon chili powder

Makes 4 servings

1. Prepare grill for direct cooking. Prepare choice of Tasty Butters.

2. Rinse lobster tails in cold water. Butterfly tails by cutting lengthwise through centers of hard top shells and meat. Cut to, but not through, bottoms of shells. Press shell halves of tails apart with fingers. Brush lobster meat with butter mixture.

3. Place tails on grid, meat side down. Grill, uncovered, over medium-high heat 4 minutes. Turn tails meat side up. Brush with butter mixture; grill 4 to 5 minutes or until lobster meat turns opaque.

4. Heat remaining butter mixture, stirring occasionally. Serve butter mixture for dipping.

Tasty Butters: For each butter sauce, combine ingredients in small bowl.

Moroccan Swordfish

4 swordfish steaks
    (4 ounces each), about
    1 inch thick
1 tablespoon fresh lemon
    juice
1 tablespoon apple cider
    vinegar
2½ teaspoons garlic-flavored
    vegetable oil
1 teaspoon ground ginger
1 teaspoon paprika
½ teaspoon ground cumin
½ teaspoon hot chili oil
¼ teaspoon salt
¼ teaspoon ground
    coriander
⅛ teaspoon black pepper
2⅔ cups hot cooked
    couscous

Makes 4 servings

1. Place swordfish in single layer in medium shallow dish. Combine lemon juice, vinegar, garlic-flavored oil, ginger, paprika, cumin, chili oil, salt, coriander and pepper in small bowl. Pour over swordfish; turn to coat both sides. Cover; refrigerate 40 minutes, turning once.

2. Prepare grill for direct cooking. Discard marinade; grill swordfish, uncovered, over medium-hot coals 8 to 10 minutes or until swordfish is opaque and flakes easily when tested with fork, turning once. Serve with couscous.

½ cup soy sauce
¼ cup lime juice
2 cloves garlic, minced
1½ pounds large shrimp, shelled and deveined
Tropical Fruit Salsa (recipe follows)
Vegetable oil
Salt and black pepper

Tropical Fruit Salsa

2 mangos*
2 kiwifruit
3 tablespoons finely chopped or finely slivered red onion
3 tablespoons lime juice
¼ teaspoon salt
⅓ teaspoon crushed red pepper flakes
1 teaspoon sugar
1 tablespoon finely chopped fresh mint leaves
1 tablespoon finely chopped fresh cilantro

Substitute 1 papaya or 2 large or 3 medium peaches for mangos.

Fish & Seafood

Shrimp Skewers with Tropical Fruit Salsa

Makes 4 servings

Combine soy sauce, lime juice and garlic in shallow glass dish or large heavy plastic food storage bag. Add shrimp; cover dish or close bag. Marinate in refrigerator no longer than 30 minutes.

Meanwhile, prepare Tropical Fruit Salsa. (Salsa should not be made more than two hours before serving.)

Remove shrimp from marinade; discard marinade. Thread shrimp on metal or bamboo skewers. (Soak bamboo skewers in water at least 20 minutes to keep them from burning.) Brush one side of shrimp lightly with oil; season with salt and pepper.

Oil hot grid to help prevent sticking. Grill shrimp, oil side down, on covered grill, over medium-hot KINGSFORD® Briquets, 6 to 8 minutes. Halfway through cooking time, brush top with oil, season with salt and pepper, then turn and continue grilling until shrimp firm up and turn opaque throughout. Serve with Tropical Fruit Salsa.

Tropical Fruit Salsa: Peel fruit. Cut mango into ¼-inch pieces; cut kiwifruit into wedges. Combine with remaining ingredients in medium bowl; adjust flavors to taste. Cover and refrigerate 2 hours.

Makes about 1 cup

Tip: Mangos are available most of the year in many large supermarkets. They are ripe when they yield to gentle pressure; color of skin does not indicate ripeness. Unripe mangos will ripen in a few days when stored at room temperature. To dice fruit, first peel skin, then cut fruit lengthwise away from seed, then cut crosswise into ¼-inch pieces.

Snapper with Pesto Butter

½ cup butter or margarine, softened
1 cup packed fresh basil leaves, coarsely chopped *or* ½ cup chopped fresh parsley plus 2 tablespoons dried basil leaves, crushed
3 tablespoons finely grated fresh Parmesan cheese
1 clove garlic, minced
Olive oil
2 to 3 teaspoons lemon juice
4 to 6 red snapper, rock cod, salmon or other medium-firm fish fillets (at least ½ inch thick)
Salt and black pepper
Lemon wedges
Fresh basil or parsley sprigs and lemon strips for garnish

Makes 4 to 6 servings

To make Pesto Butter, place butter, basil, cheese, garlic and 1 tablespoon oil in blender or food processor; process until blended. Stir in lemon juice to taste. Rinse fish; pat dry with paper towels. Brush one side of fish lightly with oil; season with salt and pepper.

Oil hot grid to help prevent sticking. Grill fillets, oil sides down, on a covered grill, over medium KINGSFORD® Briquets, 5 to 9 minutes. Halfway through cooking time, brush tops with oil; season with salt and pepper. Turn and continue grilling until fish turns opaque throughout. (Allow 3 to 5 minutes for each ½ inch of thickness.) Serve each fillet with a spoonful of Pesto Butter and a wedge of lemon. Garnish with basil sprigs and lemon strips.

Tandoori-Style Seafood Kabobs

Makes 4 servings

½ pound *each* salmon fillet, tuna steak and swordfish steak*
1 teaspoon salt
1 teaspoon ground cumin
¼ teaspoon black pepper
Dash *each* ground cinnamon, ground cloves and ground nutmeg
Dash ground cardamom (optional)
½ cup plain low-fat yogurt
¼ cup lemon juice
1 piece (1-inch cube) peeled fresh ginger, minced
1 tablespoon olive oil
2 cloves garlic, minced
½ jalapeño pepper, seeded and minced
½ pound large shrimp, shelled with tails intact, deveined
1 *each* red and green bell pepper, cut into bite-size pieces
Fresh parsley sprigs and fresh chives

Any firm fish can be substituted for any fish listed above.

Cut fish into 1½-inch cubes; cover and refrigerate. Heat salt and spices in small skillet over medium heat until fragrant (or spices may be added to marinade without heating); place spices in 2-quart glass dish. Add yogurt, lemon juice, ginger, oil, garlic and jalapeño pepper; mix well. Add fish and shrimp; turn to coat. Cover and refrigerate at least 1 hour but no longer than 2 hours. Thread a variety of seafood onto each metal or wooden skewer, alternating with bell peppers. (Soak wooden skewers in hot water 30 minutes to prevent burning.) Grill kabobs over medium-hot KINGSFORD® Briquets about 2 minutes per side until fish flakes easily when tested with fork and shrimp are pink and opaque. Remove seafood and peppers from skewers. Garnish with parsley and chives.

Fish & Seafood

Tuna Vera Cruz

3 tablespoons tequila, rum or vodka
2 tablespoons lime juice
2 teaspoons grated lime peel
1 piece (1-inch cube) fresh ginger, minced
2 cloves garlic, minced
1 teaspoon salt
1 teaspoon sugar
½ teaspoon ground cumin
¼ teaspoon ground cinnamon
¼ teaspoon black pepper
1 tablespoon vegetable oil
1½ pounds fresh tuna, halibut, swordfish or shark steaks
Lemon and lime wedges
Fresh rosemary sprigs

Makes 4 servings

Combine tequila, lime juice, lime peel, ginger, garlic, salt, sugar, cumin, cinnamon and pepper in 2-quart glass dish; stir in oil. Add tuna; turn to coat. Cover and refrigerate at least 30 minutes. Remove tuna from marinade; discard marinade. Grill tuna over medium-hot KINGSFORD® Briquets about 4 minutes per side until fish flakes when tested with fork. Garnish with lemon wedges, lime wedges and rosemary sprigs.

Fish & Seafood

Lamb

Western Lamb Riblets

5 pounds lamb riblets, cut into serving-size pieces
¾ cup bottled chili sauce
½ cup beer
½ cup honey
¼ cup Worcestershire sauce
¼ cup finely chopped onion
1 clove garlic, minced
½ teaspoon crushed red pepper flakes

Trim excess fat from riblets. In saucepan, combine chili sauce, beer, honey, Worcestershire sauce, onion, garlic and pepper flakes. Bring mixture to a boil. Reduce heat; simmer, covered, 10 minutes. Remove from heat; cool.

Place riblets in resealable plastic food storage bag. Pour cooled marinade over riblets in bag. Close bag securely and refrigerate about 2 hours, turning bag occasionally to distribute marinade evenly.

Drain riblets; reserve marinade. Arrange medium-hot KINGSFORD® Briquets around drip pan. Place riblets on grid over drip pan. Cover grill; cook 45 minutes, turning riblets and brushing with marinade twice. Bring remaining marinade to a boil; boil 1 minute. Serve with riblets.

Makes 6 servings

Lemon-Garlic Shish Kabobs

1½ pounds well-trimmed
   boneless lamb leg,
   cubed
¼ cup olive oil
2 tablespoons fresh lemon
   juice
4 cloves garlic, minced
2 tablespoons chopped
   fresh oregano *or*
   2 teaspoons dried
   oregano
½ teaspoon salt
½ teaspoon black pepper
1 red or yellow bell pepper,
   cut into 1-inch pieces
1 small zucchini, cut into
   1-inch pieces
1 yellow squash, cut into
   1-inch pieces
1 small red onion, cut into
   ½-inch wedges
8 ounces large fresh
   button mushrooms,
   wiped clean and
   stems trimmed
Fresh oregano sprigs for
   garnish

Makes 6 servings (2 kabobs each)

1. Place lamb in large resealable food storage bag. Combine oil, juice, garlic, chopped oregano, salt and black pepper in glass measuring cup; pour over lamb in bag. Close bag securely; turn to coat. Marinate lamb in refrigerator 1 to 4 hours, turning once.

2. Prepare grill for direct cooking.

3. Drain lamb, reserving marinade. Alternately thread lamb, bell pepper, zucchini, yellow squash, onion and mushrooms onto 12 (10-inch) metal skewers;* brush both sides with reserved marinade.

4. Place kabobs on grid. Grill, on covered grill, over medium-hot coals 6 minutes. Turn; continue to grill, covered, 5 to 7 minutes for medium or until desired doneness is reached. Garnish, if desired. Serve hot.

If using bamboo skewers, soak in cold water 10 to 15 minutes to prevent burning.

Herbed Lamb Chops

⅓ cup vegetable oil
⅓ cup red wine vinegar
2 tablespoons soy sauce
1 tablespoon lemon juice
3 cloves garlic, crushed
1 teaspoon chopped
 fresh oregano *or*
 ¼ teaspoon dried
 oregano
1 teaspoon dried rosemary
1 teaspoon dry mustard
1 teaspoon salt
½ teaspoon white pepper
8 lamb loin chops (about
 2 pounds), cut 1 inch
 thick

Makes 4 to 6 servings

1. Combine all ingredients except chops in large resealable food storage bag. Reserve ½ cup marinade for basting. Add chops; seal bag. Marinate in refrigerator at least 1 hour.

2. Remove chops from marinade; discard used marinade. Grill or broil chops about 8 minutes or until desired doneness, turning once and basting often with reserved ½ cup marinade. *Do not baste during last 5 minutes of cooking.* Discard any remaining marinade.

Serving Suggestion: Serve with mashed potatoes and fresh green beans.

Hint: Substitute ¼ to ½ teaspoon dried herbs for each teaspoon of fresh herbs.

Leg of Lamb with Wine Marinade

Makes 8 servings

1½ cups red wine
1 onion, chopped
1 carrot, chopped
1 stalk celery, chopped
2 tablespoons chopped fresh parsley
2 tablespoons olive oil
3 cloves garlic, minced
1 tablespoon dried thyme
1 teaspoon salt
1 teaspoon black pepper
1½ pounds boneless leg of lamb, trimmed

1. Combine all ingredients except lamb in medium bowl. Place lamb in large resealable food storage bag. Add wine mixture to bag. Close bag securely, turning to coat. Marinate in refrigerator 2 hours or overnight.

2. Prepare grill for indirect cooking. Drain lamb; reserve marinade.

3. Place lamb on grid directly over drip pan. Grill, covered, over medium heat about 45 minutes for medium or until internal temperature reaches 145°F when tested with meat thermometer inserted into thickest part of roast. Brush occasionally with reserved marinade. (Do not brush with marinade during last 5 minutes of grilling.)

4. Transfer roast to cutting board; cover with foil. Let stand 10 to 15 minutes before carving. Internal temperature will continue to rise 5°F to 10°F during stand time.

Marinated Grilled Lamb Chops

8 well-trimmed lamb loin
   chops, 1 inch thick
   (about 2¼ pounds)
3 cloves garlic, minced
2 tablespoons chopped
   fresh rosemary *or*
   2 teaspoons dried
   rosemary, crushed
2 tablespoons chopped
   fresh mint *or* 2
   teaspoons dried mint
¾ cup dry red wine
⅓ cup butter or margarine,
   softened
¼ teaspoon salt
¼ teaspoon black pepper
   Fresh mint for garnish

Makes 4 servings

1. To marinate, place chops in large resealable food storage bag. Combine garlic, rosemary and chopped mint in small bowl. Combine one-half of garlic mixture and wine in glass measuring cup. Pour wine mixture over chops in bag. Close bag securely; turn to coat. Marinate chops in refrigerator at least 2 hours or up to 4 hours, turning occasionally.

2. Add butter, salt and pepper to remaining garlic mixture; mix well. Spoon onto center of sheet of plastic wrap. Using plastic wrap as a guide, shape butter mixture into 4×1½-inch log. Wrap securely in plastic wrap; refrigerate until ready to serve.

3. Prepare grill for direct cooking. Drain chops, discarding marinade. Place chops on grid. Grill, on covered grill, over medium coals about 9 minutes or until instant-read thermometer inserted into chops registers 160°F for medium or to desired doneness, turning once.

4. Cut butter log crosswise into 8 (½-inch) slices. To serve, top each chop with slice of seasoned butter. Garnish, if desired.

1½ cups diced cucumber (about ½ pound)
1 cup plain low-fat yogurt
1 tablespoon lemon juice
1 clove garlic, minced
3 tablespoons minced fresh mint, divided
1 teaspoon salt, divided
2 green onions, chopped
2 teaspoons cornstarch
½ teaspoon ground cumin
¼ teaspoon ground cinnamon
¼ teaspoon black pepper
¼ teaspoon cayenne pepper
1 pound ground lamb,* beef or turkey
1 tablespoon olive oil**

If ground lamb is unavailable, place 1 pound boneless lamb cubes in food processor; process using on/off pulsing action until lamb is ground.

**Omit olive oil if using beef or turkey.*

Lamb

Middle Eastern Kabobs with Cucumber Sauce

Makes 4 servings

Combine cucumber, yogurt, lemon juice, garlic, 1 tablespoon mint and ½ teaspoon salt in medium bowl; cover and refrigerate ½ hour. Combine remaining 2 tablespoons mint and ½ teaspoon salt, onions, cornstarch and spices in large bowl. Add lamb and oil; mix until seasonings are well distributed. Form two 2×1½-inch oblong meatballs around each of 4 metal skewers. Grill meatballs on covered grill over medium-hot KINGSFORD® Briquets about 15 minutes until no longer pink, turning to brown all sides. Serve with cucumber sauce.

Variation: Serve kabobs in pita bread or on a sandwich roll, with cucumber sauce and thinly sliced red onion and tomato.

¼ cup Dijon mustard
2 large cloves garlic,
   minced
1 boneless butterflied leg
   of lamb (sirloin half,
   about 2½ pounds),
   well trimmed
3 tablespoons chopped
   fresh rosemary *or*
   1 tablespoon dried
   rosemary
   Fresh rosemary sprigs
   (optional)
   Mint jelly (optional)

Rosemary-Crusted Leg of Lamb

Makes 8 servings

1. Prepare grill for direct cooking.

2. Combine mustard and garlic in small bowl; spread half of mixture over one side of lamb. Sprinkle with half of chopped rosemary; pat into mustard mixture. Turn lamb over; repeat with remaining mustard mixture and rosemary. Insert meat thermometer into center of thickest part of lamb.

3. Place lamb on grid. Grill, covered, over medium coals 35 to 40 minutes or until thermometer registers 160°F for medium or until desired doneness is reached, turning every 10 minutes.

4. Meanwhile, soak rosemary sprigs in water, if desired. Place rosemary sprigs directly on coals during last 10 minutes of grilling.

5. Transfer lamb to carving board; tent with foil. Let stand 10 minutes before carving into thin slices. Serve with mint jelly, if desired.

Lamb

1 tablespoon olive oil
1 teaspoon ground cumin
1 teaspoon ground coriander
¾ teaspoon salt
⅛ teaspoon ground cinnamon
⅛ teaspoon ground red pepper
4 center-cut lamb loin chops, cut 1 inch thick (about 1 pound total)
2 cloves garlic, minced

Moroccan-Style Lamb Chops

Makes 4 servings

1. Prepare grill or preheat broiler.

2. Combine oil, cumin, coriander, salt, cinnamon and red pepper in small bowl; mix well. Rub or brush oil mixture over both sides of lamb chops. Sprinkle garlic over both sides of lamb chops. Grill on covered grill, or broil 4 to 5 inches from heat, 5 minutes per side for medium doneness.

Hint: This recipe also works well with an indoor, electric, countertop grill.

Ground Coriander

Serbian Lamb Sausage Kabobs

1 pound lean ground lamb
1 pound 90% lean ground beef
1 small onion, finely chopped
2 cloves garlic, minced
1 tablespoon hot Hungarian paprika
1 small egg, lightly beaten
Salt and black pepper to taste
3 to 4 red, green or yellow bell peppers, cut into squares
Rice pilaf for serving
Tomato slices and green onion brushes for garnish

Makes 8 servings or 16 kabobs

1. Combine lamb, beef, finely chopped onion, garlic, paprika and egg in large bowl; season with salt and black pepper.

2. Place meat mixture on cutting board; pat evenly into 8×6-inch rectangle. With sharp knife, cut meat into 48 (1-inch) squares; shape each square into small oblong sausage.

3. Place sausages on waxed paper-lined jelly-roll pan and freeze 30 to 45 minutes or until firm. Do not freeze completely. Meanwhile, prepare grill for direct grilling.

4. Alternately thread 3 sausages and 3 bell pepper pieces onto each metal skewer.

5. Grill over medium-hot coals 5 to 7 minutes. Turn kabobs, taking care not to knock sausages off. Continue grilling 5 to 7 minutes longer until meat is done. Serve with rice pilaf.

6. For green onion brushes, trim root and most of green tops from green onions. Using sharp scissors, make parallel cuts, about 1½ inches long, along length of each onion at the root end or both ends. Fan out the cuts to form a brush. If desired, place brushes in bowl of ice water for several hours to open and curl. Place green onion brush and several tomato slices on each plate, if desired.

Note: The seasonings can be adjusted, but the key to authenticity is the equal parts of beef and lamb and the garlic and paprika. You may use sweet paprika if you prefer a milder taste.

Southwestern Lamb Chops with Charred Corn Relish

Makes 4 servings

4 lamb shoulder or blade chops (about 8 ounces each), cut ¾-inch thick and well trimmed
¼ cup vegetable oil
¼ cup lime juice
1 tablespoon chili powder
2 cloves garlic, minced
1 teaspoon ground cumin
¼ teaspoon ground red pepper
Charred Corn Relish (recipe follows)
2 tablespoons chopped fresh cilantro
Hot pepper jelly (optional)

Charred Corn Relish

2 large or 3 small ears fresh corn, husked and silk removed
½ cup diced red bell pepper
¼ cup chopped fresh cilantro
3 tablespoons reserved lime juice mixture

1. Place chops in large resealable food storage bag. Combine oil, lime juice, chili powder, garlic, cumin and ground red pepper in small bowl; mix well. Reserve 3 tablespoons mixture for Charred Corn Relish; cover and refrigerate. Pour remaining mixture over chops. Close bag securely, turning to coat. Marinate in refrigerator at least 8 hours or overnight, turning occasionally.

2. Prepare grill for direct cooking. Prepare Charred Corn Relish; set aside.

3. Drain chops; discard marinade. Place chops on grid. Grill, covered, over medium heat 13 to 15 minutes for medium or until desired doneness is reached, turning halfway through grilling time. Sprinkle with cilantro. Serve with Charred Corn Relish and hot pepper jelly, if desired.

Charred Corn Relish:

1. Place corn on grid. Grill, covered, over medium heat 10 to 12 minutes or until charred, turning occasionally. Cool to room temperature.

2. Cut kernels off each cob into large bowl and press cobs with knife to release remaining corn and liquid; discard cobs.

3. Add bell pepper, cilantro and reserved lime juice mixture to corn; mix well. Let stand at room temperature while grilling chops. Cover and refrigerate if preparing in advance. Bring to room temperature before serving.

Pork

Pork and Plum Kabobs

¾ pound boneless pork loin chops (1 inch thick), trimmed of fat and cut into 1-inch pieces

1½ teaspoons ground cumin

½ teaspoon ground cinnamon

¼ teaspoon salt

¼ teaspoon garlic powder

¼ teaspoon ground red pepper

¼ cup red raspberry fruit spread

¼ cup sliced green onions

1 tablespoon orange juice

3 plums, pitted and cut into wedges

1. Place pork in large resealable food storage bag. Combine cumin, cinnamon, salt, garlic powder and red pepper in small bowl. Sprinkle over meat in bag. Shake to coat meat with spices.

2. Prepare grill for direct grilling. Combine raspberry spread, green onions and orange juice in small bowl; set aside.

3. Alternately thread pork and plum wedges onto 8 skewers.* Grill kabobs directly over medium heat 12 to 14 minutes or until meat is barely pink in center, turning once during grilling. Brush frequently with raspberry mixture during last 5 minutes of grilling.

Makes 4 servings

If using wooden skewers, soak in water 20 minutes before using to prevent burning.

Serving Suggestion: A crisp, cool salad makes a great accompaniment to these sweet grilled kabobs.

Bodacious Grilled Ribs

4 pounds pork loin back ribs
2 tablespoons paprika
2 teaspoons dried basil
½ teaspoon onion powder
¼ teaspoon garlic powder
¼ teaspoon ground red pepper
¼ teaspoon black pepper
2 sheets (24×18 inches) heavy-duty foil, lightly sprayed with nonstick cooking spray
8 ice cubes
1 cup barbecue sauce
½ cup apricot all-fruit spread

Makes 4 servings

1. Prepare grill for direct cooking. Cut ribs into 4- to 6-rib pieces.

2. Combine paprika, basil, onion powder, garlic powder, red pepper and black pepper in small bowl. Rub on both sides of rib pieces. Place 2 pounds of ribs, in single layer, in center of each foil sheet. Place 4 ice cubes on top of each.

3. Double fold sides and ends of foil to seal packets, leaving head space for heat circulation. Place on baking sheet. Stir together barbecue sauce and jam; set aside.

4. Slide packets off baking sheet onto grill grid. Grill, covered, over medium coals 45 to 60 minutes or until tender. Carefully open one end of each packet to allow steam to escape.

5. Open packets and transfer ribs to grill rack. Brush with barbecue sauce mixture. Continue grilling 5 to 10 minutes, brushing with sauce and turning often.

Cuban Garlic & Lime Pork Chops

Makes 4 servings

4 boneless pork top loin chops, ¾ inch thick (about 1½ pounds)
2 tablespoons olive oil
2 tablespoons lime juice
2 tablespoons orange juice
2 teaspoons bottled minced garlic
½ teaspoon salt, divided
½ teaspoon red pepper flakes

Salsa

2 small seedless oranges, peeled and chopped
1 medium cucumber, peeled, seeded and chopped
2 tablespoons chopped onion
2 tablespoons chopped fresh cilantro

1. Place pork in large resealable food storage bag. Add oil, juices, garlic, ¼ teaspoon salt and pepper flakes. Seal bag and shake to evenly distribute marinade; refrigerate up to 24 hours.

2. To make salsa, combine oranges, cucumber, onion and cilantro in small bowl; toss lightly. Cover and refrigerate 1 hour or overnight. Add remaining ¼ teaspoon salt just before serving.

3. To complete recipe, remove pork from marinade; discard marinade. Grill or broil pork 6 to 8 minutes on each side or until pork is no longer pink in center. Serve with salsa.

1 tablespoon chili powder
1 tablespoon dried parsley
2 teaspoons onion powder
2 teaspoons garlic powder
2 teaspoons dried oregano
2 teaspoons paprika
2 teaspoons black pepper
1½ teaspoons salt
4 pounds pork spareribs,
cut into 4 racks
Tennessee BBQ Sauce
(recipe follows)

Tennessee BBQ Sauce

3 cups prepared barbecue
sauce
¼ cup cider vinegar
¼ cup honey
2 teaspoons onion powder
2 teaspoons garlic powder
Dash hot pepper sauce

Memphis Pork Ribs

Makes 4 servings

1. Combine chili powder, parsley, onion powder, garlic powder, oregano, paprika, pepper and salt in small bowl; mix well. Rub spice mixture onto ribs. Cover; refrigerate at least 2 hours or overnight.

2. Preheat oven to 350°F. Place ribs in foil-lined shallow roasting pan. Bake 45 minutes.

3. Meanwhile, prepare grill for direct cooking. Prepare Tennessee BBQ sauce. Reserve 1 cup sauce for dipping.

4. Place ribs on grid. Grill, covered, over medium heat 10 minutes. Brush with sauce. Continue grilling 10 minutes or until ribs are tender, brushing with sauce occasionally. Serve reserved sauce on the side for dipping.

Tennessee BBQ Sauce: Combine all ingredients in medium bowl; mix well.

Makes about 3½ cups

Zesty Blue Cheese Butter (recipe follows)

4 medium baking potatoes, unpeeled

Vegetable oil

4 (¾-inch-thick) boneless pork loin chops (about 4 ounces each)

2 medium red bell peppers, cut into halves and seeded

⅓ cup butter or margarine

⅓ cup hot pepper sauce

Prepared coleslaw (optional)

Zesty Blue Cheese Butter

4 ounces blue cheese, such as Gorgonzola or Roquefort

½ cup butter or margarine, softened

1 package (3 ounces) cream cheese, softened

2 tablespoons finely chopped green onion

2 slices bacon, cooked, drained and crumbled

Fiery Grilled Buffalo-Style Chops and Vegetables

Makes 4 servings

1. Prepare Zesty Blue Cheese Butter up to 2 days in advance; refrigerate.

2. Preheat oven to 375°F. Pierce each potato several times with fork. Pat potatoes dry with paper towels; rub skins with oil. Bake 1 hour or until just fork-tender. While hot, cut potatoes lengthwise in half. Cool to room temperature.

3. Prepare grill for direct cooking.

4. Place pork chops, bell peppers and potatoes in large resealable food storage bag. Melt butter in small saucepan over low heat. Stir in pepper sauce; pour over chops, bell peppers and potatoes. Seal bag tightly; turn to coat. Marinate at room temperature no more than 15 minutes, turning once.

5. Place chops and vegetables on grid, reserving marinade in small saucepan. Grill, uncovered, over medium coals 5 minutes. Turn chops and vegetables and baste once with reserved marinade; discard any remaining marinade. Cook 5 minutes more or until pork is barely pink in center. (Do not overcook.)

6. Serve chops and vegetables with slices of Zesty Blue Cheese Butter.

Zesty Blue Cheese Butter

1. Crumble blue cheese with fingers to measure 1 cup; place in small bowl.

2. Add butter and cream cheese; beat with electric mixer at medium speed until smooth. Stir in onion and bacon.

3. Place butter mixture on sheet of waxed paper. Using waxed paper, roll mixture back and forth into 8-inch log.

4. Wrap waxed paper around butter log to seal. Refrigerate at least 1 hour or up to 2 days.

¾ cup apricot preserves
¾ cup Dijon mustard
1 pound smoked andouille
or other pork sausage,
cut into 1½-inch pieces
16 dried apricot halves
16 medium whole
mushrooms

Grilled Sausage Kabobs with Apricot Mustard Sauce

Makes 4 servings

1. Prepare grill for direct grilling. Combine preserves and mustard in small bowl; mix well.

2. Thread sausage, apricots and mushrooms onto 4 skewers. Brush with one-quarter of preserve mixture.

3. Grill over medium-hot coals 8 minutes, turning once. Baste with one-half of preserve mixture and continue grilling 2 minutes more, turning once, or until sausage is lightly browned. Serve kabobs with remaining one-quarter of preserve mixture for dipping.

Hint: Andouille sausage is a spicy, smoked pork sausage often used in Cajun and Creole cooking. It makes a delicious addition to many other dishes.

Pork Chops with Apple-Sage Stuffing

Makes 6 servings

6 center-cut pork chops (3 pounds), about 1 inch thick
¾ cup dry vermouth, divided
4 tablespoons minced fresh sage *or* 4 teaspoons rubbed sage, divided
2 tablespoons soy sauce
1 tablespoon olive oil
2 cloves garlic, minced
½ teaspoon black pepper, divided
1 tablespoon butter
1 medium onion, diced
1 apple, cored and diced
½ teaspoon salt
2 cups fresh firm-textured white bread crumbs
Curly endive
Plum slices

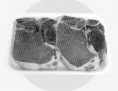

Cut pocket in each chop using tip of thin, sharp knife. Combine ¼ cup vermouth, 2 tablespoons fresh sage (or 2 teaspoons rubbed sage), soy sauce, oil, garlic and ¼ teaspoon pepper in glass dish; add pork chops, turning to coat. Heat butter in large skillet over medium heat until foamy. Add onion and apple; cook and stir about 6 minutes until onion is tender. Stir in remaining ½ cup vermouth, 2 tablespoons sage, ¼ teaspoon pepper and salt. Cook and stir over high heat about 3 minutes until liquid is almost gone. Transfer onion mixture to large bowl. Stir in bread crumbs.

Remove pork chops from marinade; discard marinade. Spoon onion mixture into pockets of pork chops. Close openings with wooden picks. (Soak wooden picks in hot water 15 minutes to prevent burning.) Grill pork chops on covered grill over medium KINGSFORD® Briquets about 5 minutes per side until barely pink in center. Garnish with endive and plum slices.

Pork Tenderloin with Grilled Apple Cream Sauce

Makes 4 servings

- 1 can (6 ounces) frozen apple juice concentrate, thawed and divided (¾ cup)
- ½ cup Calvados or brandy, divided
- 2 tablespoons Dijon mustard
- 1 tablespoon olive oil
- 3 cloves garlic, minced
- 1¼ teaspoons salt, divided
- ¼ teaspoon black pepper
- 1½ pounds pork tenderloin
- 2 green or red apples, cored
- 1 tablespoon butter
- ½ large red onion, cut into thin slivers
- ½ cup heavy cream
  Fresh thyme sprigs

Reserve 2 tablespoons juice concentrate. Combine remaining juice concentrate, ¼ cup Calvados, mustard, oil, garlic, 1 teaspoon salt and pepper in glass dish. Add pork; turn to coat. Cover and refrigerate 2 hours, turning pork occasionally. Cut apples crosswise into ⅜-inch rings. Remove pork from marinade; discard marinade. Grill pork on covered grill over medium KINGSFORD® Briquets about 20 minutes, turning 3 times, until meat thermometer inserted in thickest part registers 155°F. Grill apples about 4 minutes per side until tender; cut rings into quarters. Melt butter in large skillet over medium heat. Add onion; cook and stir until soft. Stir in apples, remaining ¼ cup Calvados, ¼ teaspoon salt and reserved 2 tablespoons juice concentrate. Add cream; heat through. Cut pork crosswise into ½-inch slices; spoon sauce over pork. Garnish with fresh thyme.

1 cup peach jam
2 tablespoons cider
    vinegar
1 tablespoon chopped
    fresh parsley
1 tablespoon brown sugar
2 cloves garlic, minced
½ teaspoon black pepper
4 ham steaks (about
    5 ounces each)

Sweet and Sour Ham Steaks

Makes 4 servings

1. Prepare grill for direct cooking.

2. Combine jam, vinegar, parsley, brown sugar, garlic and pepper in small bowl; mix well.

3. Place ham steaks on grid. Brush with jam mixture. Grill over medium-high heat 4 minutes. Turn ham steaks and brush with jam mixture. Grill 4 minutes.

4. Serve ham steaks with remaining jam mixture on the side.

2 cups orange juice
⅓ cup lime juice
⅓ cup packed brown sugar
3 medium oranges,
    peeled, seeded and
    cut into ¼-inch pieces
¼ cup chopped red onion
¼ cup diced radishes
2 tablespoons finely
    chopped fresh cilantro
6 pork chops (about
    ¾-inch thick)
Salt and black pepper
Orange curls and
    radishes for garnish

Pork Chops with Orange-Radish Relish

Makes 6 servings

Combine both juices and brown sugar in saucepan. Cook mixture at a low boil, stirring often, about 20 minutes until reduced to about ½ cup and it has a syruplike consistency. Set aside ¼ cup sauce for basting.

Meanwhile, prepare Orange-Radish Relish by combining oranges, onion and diced radishes in colander or strainer and drain well; transfer to bowl. Add cilantro and gently stir in remaining orange syrup. Season pork with salt and pepper.

Oil hot grid to help prevent sticking. Grill pork, on covered grill, over medium KINGSFORD® Briquets, 7 to 10 minutes. (Pork is done at 160°F; it should be juicy and slightly pink in center.) Halfway through cooking, brush with reserved ¼ cup orange syrup and turn once. Serve with Orange-Radish Relish. Garnish with orange curls and radishes.

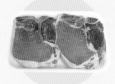

Sandwiches & Burgers

Bratwurst Sandwiches

1 bottle or can (12 ounces) beer
4 fresh bratwurst (about 1 pound)
1 medium onion, sliced
1 small red bell pepper, cut lengthwise into thin strips
1 small green bell pepper, cut lengthwise into thin strips
1 tablespoon olive oil
¾ teaspoon salt
½ teaspoon black pepper
4 hoagie or submarine sandwich rolls, split
Spicy brown or Dijon mustard
Hot sport peppers (optional)

1. Combine beer and bratwurst in medium saucepan; bring to boil over high heat. Reduce heat; simmer uncovered 20 to 25 minutes or until bratwurst are no longer pink in center, turning occasionally. Cool in liquid. Drain bratwurst; wrap in foil or plastic food storage bag. Refrigerate up to 24 hours.*

2. Combine onion and bell peppers on large sheet of heavy aluminum foil. Drizzle oil and sprinkle salt and pepper over vegetables. Place another sheet of foil over vegetables; fold up all edges of foil, forming a packet. Refrigerate up to 24 hours.

3. Prepare grill for direct cooking. Place foil packet on grid over medium coals. Cook 5 minutes. Place bratwursts on grid and turn vegetable packet over. Continue grilling 10 minutes or until bratwursts are heated through and vegetables are tender, turning bratwursts and foil packet once.

4. Place rolls, split sides down, on grid to toast lightly during last 1 to 2 minutes of grilling. Serve bratwursts in rolls topped with vegetables from foil packet. Serve with mustard and hot peppers, if desired.

*If tailgating, wrap and refrigerate to transport foods safely to tailgating site. For backyard grilling, wrapping is unnecessary. Cook as directed.

Makes 6 servings

Cilantro Pesto

1 large clove garlic
4 ounces fresh cilantro, stems removed and rinsed
1½ teaspoons bottled minced jalapeño pepper *or* 1 tablespoon bottled sliced jalapeño pepper,* drained
¼ teaspoon salt
¼ cup vegetable oil

Burgers

1¼ pounds ground beef
¼ cup plus 1 tablespoon Cilantro Pesto, divided
½ teaspoon salt
4 slices pepper Jack cheese
2 tablespoons light or regular mayonnaise
4 kaiser rolls, split
1 ripe avocado, peeled and sliced
Salsa

*Jalapeño peppers can sting and irritate the skin, so wear rubber gloves when handling peppers and do not touch your eyes.

Southwest Pesto Burgers

Makes 4 servings

1. For pesto, with motor running, drop garlic through feed tube of food processor; process until minced. Add cilantro, jalapeño pepper and salt; process until cilantro is chopped.

2. With motor running, slowly add oil through feed tube; process until thick paste forms. Transfer to container with tight-fitting lid. Refrigerate until needed.

3. To complete recipe, prepare barbecue grill for direct cooking.

4. Combine beef, ¼ cup pesto and salt in large bowl; mix well. Form into 4 patties. Place patties on grid over medium heat. Grill 8 to 10 minutes covered or 13 to 15 minutes uncovered to medium (160°F), turning once. Top patties with cheese during final minute of grilling.

5. While patties are cooking, combine mayonnaise and remaining 1 tablespoon pesto in small bowl; mix well. Top patties with mayonnaise mixture. Serve on rolls with avocado and salsa.

Serving Suggestion: Serve with refried beans.

Pesto Chicken & Pepper Wraps

Makes 5 wraps

⅔ cup refrigerated or frozen pesto sauce, thawed and divided

3 tablespoons red wine vinegar

¼ teaspoon salt

¼ teaspoon black pepper

1¼ pounds boneless, skinless chicken thighs or breasts

2 red bell peppers, cut in half, stemmed and seeded

5 (8-inch) flour tortillas

5 thin slices (3-inch rounds) fresh-pack mozzarella cheese*

5 leaves Boston or red leaf lettuce

Orange slices

Red and green chilies

Fresh basil sprigs

Packaged sliced whole milk or part-skim mozzarella cheese can be substituted for fresh-pack mozzarella cheese.

Combine ¼ cup pesto, vinegar, salt and black pepper in medium bowl. Add chicken; toss to coat. Cover and refrigerate at least 30 minutes. Remove chicken from marinade; discard marinade. Grill chicken over medium-hot KINGSFORD® Briquets about 4 minutes per side until chicken is no longer pink in center, turning once. Grill bell peppers, skin sides down, about 8 minutes until skin is charred. Place bell peppers in large resealable plastic food storage bag; seal. Let stand 5 minutes; remove skin. Cut chicken and bell peppers into thin strips. Spread about 1 tablespoon of remaining pesto down center of each tortilla; top with chicken, bell peppers, cheese and lettuce. Roll tortillas to enclose filling. Garnish with orange slices, chilies and basil sprigs.

Blue Cheese Burgers with Red Onion

Makes 6 servings

2 pounds ground beef chuck
2 cloves garlic, minced
1 teaspoon salt
½ teaspoon black pepper
4 ounces blue cheese
⅓ cup coarsely chopped walnuts, toasted
1 torpedo (long) red onion *or* 2 small red onions, sliced into ⅜-inch-thick rounds
2 baguettes (each 12 inches long)
Olive or vegetable oil

Combine beef, garlic, salt and pepper in medium bowl. Shape meat mixture into 12 oval patties. Mash cheese and blend with walnuts in small bowl. Divide cheese mixture equally; place on centers of 6 meat patties. Top with remaining meat patties; tightly pinch edges together to seal in filling.

Oil hot grid to help prevent sticking. Grill patties and onion, if desired, on covered grill, over medium KINGSFORD® Briquets, 7 to 12 minutes for medium doneness (160°F), turning once. Cut baguettes into 4-inch lengths; split each piece and brush cut side with olive oil. Move cooked burgers to edge of grill to keep warm. Grill bread, oil side down, until lightly toasted. Serve burgers on toasted baguettes.

Fish Tacos with Yogurt Sauce

Sauce

- ½ cup plain yogurt
- 1 tablespoon mayonnaise
- 3 tablespoons sour cream
- ½ teaspoon ground cumin
- ¼ teaspoon cayenne pepper
- Juice of 1 lime
- ¼ cup chopped cilantro
- Salt and black pepper

Tacos

- Juice of ½ lime
- 2 tablespoons canola oil
- 1½ pounds swordfish, halibut or tilapia fillets
- Salt and ground black pepper
- 12 corn or flour tortillas
- 3 cups shredded cabbage or prepared coleslaw mixture
- 2 medium tomatoes, chopped

Makes 6 servings

1. For sauce: In a small bowl, mix all sauce ingredients. Season with salt and pepper to taste.

2. For tacos: Preheat grill. In a cup or small bowl, combine lime juice and oil. About 5 minutes before cooking, brush or spoon lime and oil mixture over fish fillets and season with salt and pepper to taste. (Do not marinate fish longer than about 5 minutes, or acid in lime will begin to "cook" fish.)

3. Spray grid or grill basket with nonstick cooking spray. Grill fish 5 minutes; turn fish and cover grill. Cook 5 minutes more; remove from grill. Flake fish or break into large pieces, if desired.

4. Place tortillas on grill or on burner over medium heat 10 seconds on each side or until beginning to bubble and brown lightly. Fill tortillas with fish. Top with sauce, cabbage and tomatoes.

½ cup ketchup
⅓ cup packed brown sugar
2 tablespoons bourbon
   or whiskey (optional)
1 tablespoon
   Worcestershire sauce
½ teaspoon dry mustard
¼ teaspoon ground red
   pepper
1 clove garlic, minced
2 whole pork tenderloins
   (about ¾ pound each),
   well trimmed of fat
1 large red onion, cut into
   6 (¼-inch-thick) slices
6 hoagie rolls or kaiser
   rolls, split

Barbecued Pork Tenderloin Sandwiches

Makes 6 servings

1. Prepare grill for direct cooking.

2. Combine ketchup, sugar, bourbon, if desired, Worcestershire sauce, mustard, red pepper and garlic in small, heavy saucepan with ovenproof handle; mix well. Set saucepan on one side of grid.*

3. Place tenderloins on center of grid. Grill tenderloins on uncovered grill over medium-hot coals 8 minutes. Simmer sauce 5 minutes or until thickened, stirring occasionally.

4. Turn tenderloins with tongs; continue to grill, uncovered, 5 minutes. Add onion slices to grid. Set aside half of sauce; reserve. Brush tenderloins and onion with remaining sauce.

5. Continue to grill, uncovered, 7 to 10 minutes or until internal temperature reaches 160°F when tested with meat thermometer inserted into thickest part of tenderloins.**

6. Transfer roast to cutting board; cover with foil. Let stand 10 to 15 minutes before carving. Internal temperature will continue to rise 5°F to 10°F during stand time. Carve tenderloins crosswise into thin slices. Separate onion slices into rings. Divide meat and onion rings among rolls; drizzle with reserved sauce.

If desired, sauce may be prepared on range-top. Combine ketchup, sugar, bourbon, if desired, Worcestershire sauce, mustard, ground red pepper and garlic in small saucepan. Bring to a boil over medium-high heat. Reduce heat to low and simmer, uncovered, 5 minutes or until thickened, stirring occasionally.

**If using an instant-read thermometer, do not leave thermometer in tenderloin during grilling since thermometer is not heatproof.*

Grilled Chile Chicken Quesadillas

2 tablespoons lime juice
3 cloves garlic, minced
1 tablespoon ground
   cumin
1 tablespoon chili powder
1 tablespoon vegetable oil
1 jalapeño pepper, minced
1 teaspoon salt
6 skinless boneless chicken
   thighs
3 poblano peppers, cut in
   half, stemmed, seeded
2 avocados, peeled and
   sliced
3 cups (12 ounces)
   shredded Monterey
   Jack cheese
12 (8-inch) flour tortillas
1½ cups fresh salsa
   Red chiles
   Fresh cilantro sprigs

Makes 12 quesadillas

Combine lime juice, garlic, cumin, chili powder, oil, jalapeño pepper and salt in small bowl; coat chicken with paste. Cover and refrigerate chicken at least 15 minutes. Grill chicken on covered grill over medium-hot KINGSFORD® Briquets 4 minutes per side until no longer pink in center. Grill poblano peppers, skin side down, 8 minutes until skins are charred. Place peppers in large resealable plastic food storage bag; seal. Let stand 5 minutes; remove skin. Cut chicken and peppers into strips. Arrange chicken, peppers, avocado and cheese on half of each tortilla. Drizzle with 2 tablespoons salsa. Fold other half of tortilla over filling. Grill quesadillas on covered grill over medium briquets 30 seconds to 1 minute per side until cheese is melted. Garnish with chiles and cilantro sprigs.

¼ cup pine nuts
1 pound ground lamb
¼ cup finely chopped
   yellow onion
3 cloves garlic, minced,
   divided
¾ teaspoon salt
¼ teaspoon black pepper
¼ cup plain yogurt
¼ teaspoon sugar
4 slices red onion (¼ inch
   thick)
1 tablespoon olive oil
8 pumpernickel bread
   slices
12 thin cucumber slices
4 tomato slices

Greek Lamb Burgers

Makes 4 servings

1. Prepare grill for direct cooking. Meanwhile, heat small skillet over medium heat until hot. Add pine nuts; cook 30 to 45 seconds until light brown, shaking pan occasionally.

2. Combine lamb, pine nuts, yellow onion, 2 cloves garlic, salt and pepper in large bowl; mix well. Shape mixture into 4 patties, about ½ inch thick and 4 inches in diameter. Combine yogurt, sugar and remaining 1 clove garlic in small bowl; set aside.

3. Brush 1 side of each patty and red onion slice with oil; place on grid, oiled sides down. Brush tops with oil. Grill, on covered grill, over medium-hot coals 8 to 10 minutes for medium or to desired doneness, turning halfway through grilling time. Place bread on grid to toast during last few minutes of grilling time; grill 1 to 2 minutes per side.

4. Top 4 bread slices with patties and red onion slices; top each with 3 cucumber slices and 1 tomato slice. Dollop evenly with yogurt mixture. Top sandwiches with remaining 4 bread slices. Serve immediately.

Turkey Burritos

1 tablespoon ground cumin
1 tablespoon chili powder
1½ teaspoons salt
1½ to 2 pounds turkey tenderloin, cut into ½-inch cubes
Avocado-Corn Salsa (recipe follows, optional)
Lime wedges
Flour tortillas
Sour cream (optional)
Tomato slices for garnish

Avocado-Corn Salsa

2 small to medium-size ripe avocados, finely chopped
1 cup cooked fresh corn or thawed frozen corn
2 medium tomatoes, seeded and finely chopped
2 to 3 tablespoons chopped fresh cilantro
2 to 3 tablespoons lime juice
½ to 1 teaspoon minced hot green chili pepper
½ teaspoon salt

Makes 6 servings

Combine cumin, chili powder and salt in cup. Place turkey cubes in a shallow glass dish or large heavy plastic bag; pour dry rub over turkey and coat turkey thoroughly. Let turkey stand while preparing Avocado-Corn Salsa. Thread turkey onto metal or bamboo skewers. (Soak bamboo skewers in water at least 20 minutes before using to prevent them from burning.)

Oil hot grid to help prevent sticking. Grill turkey, on a covered grill, over medium KINGSFORD® Briquets, about 6 minutes or until turkey is no longer pink in center, turning once. Remove skewers from grill; squeeze lime wedges over skewers. Warm flour tortillas in microwave oven, or brush each tortilla very lightly with water and grill 10 to 15 seconds per side. Top with Avocado-Corn Salsa and sour cream, if desired. Garnish with tomato slices.

Avocado-Corn Salsa: Gently stir together all ingredients in medium bowl; adjust flavors to taste. Cover and refrigerate until ready to serve.

Makes about 1½ cups

Tip: This recipe is great for casual get-togethers. Just prepare the fixings and let the guests make their own burritos.

Vietnamese Grilled Steak Wraps

1 beef flank steak (about 1½ pounds)
Grated peel and juice of 2 lemons
6 tablespoons sugar, divided
2 tablespoons dark sesame oil
1¼ teaspoons salt, divided
½ teaspoon black pepper
¼ cup water
¼ cup rice vinegar
½ teaspoon crushed red pepper
6 (8-inch) flour tortillas
6 red leaf lettuce leaves
⅓ cup lightly packed fresh mint leaves
⅓ cup lightly packed fresh cilantro leaves
Star fruit slices
Red bell pepper strips
Orange peel strips

Makes 6 wraps

Cut beef across the grain into thin slices. Combine lemon peel, juice, 2 tablespoons sugar, sesame oil, 1 teaspoon salt and black pepper in medium bowl. Add beef; toss to coat. Cover and refrigerate at least 30 minutes. Combine water, vinegar, remaining 4 tablespoons sugar and ¼ teaspoon salt in small saucepan; bring to a boil. Boil 5 minutes without stirring until syrupy. Stir in crushed red pepper; set aside.

Remove beef from marinade; discard marinade. Thread beef onto metal or wooden skewers. (Soak wooden skewers in hot water 30 minutes to prevent burning.) Grill beef over medium-hot KINGSFORD® Briquets about 3 minutes per side until cooked through. Grill tortillas until hot. Place lettuce, beef, mint and cilantro on tortillas; drizzle with vinegar mixture. Roll tortillas to enclose filling. Garnish with star fruit, bell pepper and orange peel strips.

Salads

Basil Vinaigrette (recipe follows)
1 pound asparagus, trimmed
1¼ teaspoons salt, divided
1 pound salmon fillets
1½ teaspoons olive oil
¼ teaspoon black pepper
4 lemon wedges

Basil Vinaigrette
3 tablespoons extra-virgin olive oil
1 tablespoon white wine vinegar
1 tablespoon minced fresh basil
1 small clove garlic, minced
1 teaspoon minced fresh chives
⅛ teaspoon salt
¼ teaspoon black pepper

Salmon Salad with Basil Vinaigrette

1. Prepare Basil Vinaigrette. Preheat grill to medium-hot. Place 3 inches of water and 1 teaspoon salt in large saucepan or Dutch oven. Bring to boil over high heat. Add asparagus; boil gently 6 to 8 minutes or until asparagus is crisp-tender; drain and set aside.

2. Brush salmon with olive oil. Sprinkle with remaining ¼ teaspoon salt and pepper. Grill on well-oiled grid over medium-hot coals 4 or 5 minutes per side or until fish just begins to flake when tested with a fork.

3. Remove skin from salmon. Break salmon into bite-size pieces. Arrange salmon over asparagus spears on serving plate. Spoon Basil Vinaigrette over salmon. Serve with lemon wedges.

Basil Vinaigrette: Combine all ingredients in small bowl; stir until blended.

Makes 4 servings

½ cup fat-free mayonnaise
2 tablespoons cider vinegar
  or white wine vinegar
1 tablespoon spicy brown
  mustard
2 cloves garlic, minced
½ teaspoon sugar
6 cups torn assorted
  lettuces such as
  romaine, red leaf and
  Bibb
1 large tomato, seeded
  and chopped
⅓ cup chopped fresh basil
2 slices red onion,
  separated into rings
1 boneless beef top sirloin
  steak (about 1 pound)
½ teaspoon salt
½ teaspoon black pepper
½ cup herb or garlic
  croutons
  Additional black pepper
  (optional)

Grilled Beef Salad

Makes 4 servings

1. Prepare grill for direct cooking. Combine mayonnaise, vinegar, mustard, garlic and sugar in small bowl; mix well. Cover and refrigerate until serving.

2. Toss together lettuce, tomato, basil and onion in large bowl; cover and refrigerate until serving.

3. Sprinkle both sides of steak with salt and black pepper. Place steak on grid. Grill, uncovered, over medium heat 13 to 16 minutes for medium-rare to medium or until desired doneness, turning once.

4. Transfer steak to carving board. Slice in half lengthwise; carve crosswise into thin slices.

5. Add steak and croutons to bowl with lettuce mixture; toss well. Add mayonnaise mixture; toss until well coated. Serve with additional black pepper, if desired.

6 ounces turkey breast tenderloin
1½ teaspoons Caribbean jerk seasoning
4 cups mixed salad greens
¾ cup sliced peeled cucumber
⅔ cup chopped fresh pineapple
⅔ cup quartered strawberries or raspberries
½ cup slivered peeled jicama or sliced celery
1 green onion, sliced
¼ cup lime juice
3 tablespoons honey

Jerk Turkey Salad

Makes 2 servings

1. Prepare grill for direct grilling. Rub turkey with jerk seasoning.

2. Grill turkey over medium coals 15 to 20 minutes or until turkey is no longer pink in center and juices run clear, turning once. Remove from grill and cool.

3. Cut turkey into bite-size pieces. Toss together turkey, greens, cucumber, pineapple, strawberries, jicama and green onion.

4. Combine lime juice and honey. Toss with greens mixture. Serve immediately.

¼ cup cider vinegar
¼ cup extra-virgin olive oil
   Grated peel and juice of
   1 lemon
4 teaspoons Dijon mustard,
   divided
1 clove garlic, minced
¼ teaspoon salt
¼ teaspoon black pepper
2 teaspoons minced
   fresh tarragon *or*
   ¾ teaspoon dried
   tarragon leaves
1 pound small salmon
   fillets, skinned
1 medium red onion,
   thinly sliced
1 pound asparagus, ends
   trimmed
¼ pound shiitake
   mushrooms or
   button mushrooms
   Additional salt and black
   pepper
8 cups lightly packed torn
   romaine and red leaf
   lettuce

Salmon, Asparagus and Shiitake Salad

Makes 4 main-dish servings

Combine vinegar, oil, peel, juice, 2 teaspoons mustard, garlic, ¼ teaspoon salt and ¼ teaspoon pepper in medium bowl; spoon 3 tablespoons dressing into 2-quart glass dish to use as marinade. Reserve remaining dressing. Add tarragon and 2 teaspoons remaining mustard to marinade in glass dish; blend well. Add salmon; turn to coat. Cover and refrigerate 1 hour. Transfer 3 tablespoons reserved dressing to medium bowl; add onion, tossing to coat. Thread asparagus and mushrooms onto wooden skewers. (Soak skewers in hot water 30 minutes to prevent burning.)

Remove salmon from marinade; discard marinade. Season salmon to taste with additional salt and pepper. Lightly oil hot grid to prevent sticking. Grill salmon over medium-hot KINGSFORD® Briquets 2 to 4 minutes per side or until fish flakes when tested with fork. Grill asparagus and mushrooms over medium-hot briquets 5 to 8 minutes or until crisp-tender. Cut asparagus into 2-inch pieces and slice mushrooms; add to onion mixture. Let stand 10 minutes. Toss lettuce with onion mixture in large bowl; arrange lettuce on platter. Break salmon into 2-inch pieces; arrange salmon and vegetables over lettuce. Drizzle with remaining reserved dressing. Serve immediately.

Chili-Crusted Grilled Chicken Caesar Salad

1 to 2 lemons
1 tablespoon minced garlic, divided
1½ teaspoons dried oregano leaves, crushed, divided
1 teaspoon chili powder
1 pound boneless skinless chicken breasts
1 tablespoon olive oil
2 anchovy fillets, minced
1 large head romaine lettuce, cut into 1-inch strips
¼ cup grated Parmesan cheese
4 whole wheat pita breads or whole wheat rolls

Makes 4 servings

1. Grate lemon peel; measure 1 to 2 teaspoons. Juice lemon; measure ¼ cup. Combine lemon peel and 1 tablespoon juice in small bowl. Set ¼ teaspoon garlic aside. Add remaining garlic, 1 teaspoon oregano and chili powder to lemon peel mixture; stir to combine. Rub chicken with lemon peel mixture.

2. Combine remaining 3 tablespoons lemon juice, ¼ teaspoon garlic, remaining ½ teaspoon oregano, oil and anchovies in large bowl. Add lettuce; toss to coat. Sprinkle with cheese; toss.

3. Spray cold grid with nonstick cooking spray. Prepare grill for direct grilling. Place chicken on grid 3 to 4 inches above medium-hot coals. Grill chicken 5 to 6 minutes. Turn chicken; grill 3 to 4 minutes or until chicken is no longer pink in center.

4. Arrange salad on 4 large plates. Slice chicken; fan on each salad. Serve with pita breads.

Sausage & Wilted Spinach Salad

Makes 4 servings

¼ cup sherry vinegar or white wine vinegar
1 teaspoon whole mustard seeds, crushed
½ teaspoon salt
¼ teaspoon black pepper
2 ears corn, husked
1 large red onion, cut into ¾-inch-thick slices
4 tablespoons extra-virgin olive oil, divided
12 ounces smoked turkey, chicken or pork sausage links, such as Polish, andouille or New Mexico style, cut in half lengthwise
2 cloves garlic, minced
10 cups lightly packed spinach leaves, torn
1 large avocado, peeled and cubed

Combine vinegar, mustard seeds, salt and pepper; set dressing aside. Brush corn and onion with 1 tablespoon oil. Insert wooden picks into onion slices from edges to prevent separating into rings. (Soak wooden picks in hot water 15 minutes to prevent burning.) Grill sausage, corn and onion over medium KINGSFORD® Briquets 6 to 10 minutes until vegetables are crisp-tender and sausage is hot, turning several times. Cut corn kernels from cobs; chop onion and slice sausage. Heat remaining 3 tablespoons oil in small skillet over medium heat. Add garlic; cook and stir 1 minute. Toss spinach, avocado, sausage, corn, onion and dressing in large bowl. Drizzle hot oil mixture over salad; toss and serve immediately.

Index

A

Appetizers

Chicken Ribbons Satay 58
Grilled Lobster, Shrimp and Calamari
        Seviche. 20
Herbed Mushroom Vegetable
        Medley 12
Italian Grilled Vegetables. 8
Portobello Mushrooms Sesame. 14
Roasted Eggplant Dip 18
Western Lamb Riblets. 84

B

Barbecued Pork Tenderloin
        Sandwiches 134

Beef

Beef with Dry Spice Rub. 34
Blue Cheese Burgers with
        Red Onion. 130
Ginger Beef and Carrot Kabobs 24
Grilled Beef Salad 146
Guadalajara Beef and Salsa. 36
Jamaican Steak 26
Middle Eastern Kabobs with
        Cucumber Sauce. 94
Rosemary Steak. 42
Serbian Lamb Sausage Kabobs 100
Skewered Beef Strips with Spicy
        Honey Glaze 38
Southwest Pesto Burgers 126
Spicy Smoked Beef Ribs 32
Teriyaki Glazed Beef Kabobs. 28
Texas Beef Brisket 30
Vietnamese Grilled Steak Wraps. 142

Beef with Dry Spice Rub 34
Blue Cheese Burgers with Red Onion 130

Bodacious Grilled Ribs 106
Bratwurst Sandwiches. 124

C

Cajun Grilled Shrimp. 66

Chicken

Chicken Ribbons Satay 58
Chili-Crusted Grilled Chicken
        Caesar Salad 152
Citrus Marinated Chicken 62
Classic Grilled Chicken 50
Glazed Cornish Hens 44
Grilled Chile Chicken Quesadillas 136
Herb Garlic Grilled Chicken 46
Lemon Herbed Chicken 56
Mediterranean Chicken Kabobs 48
Pesto Chicken & Pepper Wraps 128
Sausage & Wilted Spinach Salad 154
Southwest Chicken. 52
Thai Barbecued Chicken. 54

Chicken Ribbons Satay 58
Chili-Crusted Grilled Chicken
        Caesar Salad 152
Citrus Marinated Chicken. 62
Classic Grilled Chicken. 50
Cuban Garlic & Lime Pork Chops 108

D-F

Fiery Grilled Buffalo-Style Chops
        and Vegetables. 112

Fish

Fish Tacos with Yogurt Sauce. 132
Grilled Fish Steaks with Tomato
        Basil Butter Sauce. 68
Grilled Fish with Buttery Lemon
        Parsley 64
Grilled Fish with Orange-Chile Salsa. 70
Moroccan Swordfish. 74
Salmon, Asparagus and Shiitake Salad 150

Fish, (continued)

Salmon Salad with Basil
Vinaigrette 144
Snapper with Pesto Butter. 78
Tandoori-Style Seafood Kabobs 80
Tuna Vera Cruz 82

Fish Tacos with Yogurt Sauce 132

G

Ginger Beef and Carrot Kabobs. 24
Glazed Cornish Hens. 44
Greek Lamb Burgers 138
Grilled Beef Salad 146
Grilled Cajun Potato Wedges. 10
Grilled Chile Chicken Quesadillas 136
Grilled Fish Steaks with Tomato
Basil Butter Sauce 68
Grilled Fish with Buttery Lemon
Parsley 64
Grilled Fish with Orange-Chile Salsa 70
Grilled Lobster, Shrimp and
Calamari Seviche 20
Grilled Sausage Kabobs with
Apricot Mustard Sauce. 114
Guadalajara Beef and Salsa 36

H

Herb Garlic Grilled Chicken 46
Herbed Lamb Chops 88
Herbed Mushroom Vegetable
Medley. 12

I

Italian Grilled Vegetables. 8

J-K

Jamaican Steak 26
Jerk Turkey Salad. 148

L

Lamb

Greek Lamb Burgers. 138

Herbed Lamb Chops 88
Leg of Lamb with Wine Marinade 90
Lemon-Garlic Shish Kabobs 86
Marinated Grilled Lamb Chops 92
Middle Eastern Kabobs with
Cucumber Sauce. 94
Moroccan-Style Lamb Chops 98
Rosemary-Crusted Leg of Lamb 96
Serbian Lamb Sausage Kabobs 100
Southwestern Lamb Chops with
Charred Corn Relish 102
Western Lamb Riblets. 84

Leg of Lamb with Wine Marinade 90
Lemon Herbed Chicken 56
Lemon-Garlic Shish Kabobs 86
Lobster Tails with Tasty Butters 72

M

Marinated Grilled Lamb Chops 92
Mediterranean Chicken Kabobs 48
Memphis Pork Ribs 110
Middle Eastern Kabobs with
Cucumber Sauce 94
Moroccan Swordfish 74
Moroccan-Style Lamb Chops 98

Mushroom

Grilled Sausage Kabobs with
Apricot Mustard Sauce 114
Herbed Mushroom Vegetable
Medley 12
Lemon-Garlic Shish Kabobs 86
Mediterranean Chicken Kabobs 48
Portobello Mushrooms Sesame. 14
Salmon, Asparagus and Shiitake
Salad 150
Turkey Teriyaki with Grilled
Mushrooms. 60

N-P

Parmesan Polenta 22
Pesto Chicken & Pepper Wraps 128

Pork

Barbecued Pork Tenderloin
  Sandwiches. 134
Bodacious Grilled Ribs 106
Bratwurst Sandwiches 124
Cuban Garlic & Lime Pork Chops 108
Fiery Grilled Buffalo-Style Chops
  and Vegetables. 112
Grilled Beef Salad 146
Grilled Sausage Kabobs with
  Apricot Mustard Sauce 114
Memphis Pork Ribs. 110
Pork and Plum Kabobs. 104
Pork Chops with Apple-Sage
  Stuffing 116
Pork Chops with Orange-Radish
  Relish 122
Pork Tenderloin with Grilled
  Apple Cream Sauce 118
Sausage & Wilted Spinach Salad. 154
Sweet and Sour Ham Steaks 120
Pork and Plum Kabobs 104
Pork Chops with Apple-Sage
  Stuffing 116
Pork Chops with Orange-Radish
  Relish 122
Pork Tenderloin with Grilled
  Apple Cream Sauce 118
Portobello Mushrooms Sesame 14

Q-R
Ribs

Bodacious Grilled Ribs 106
Memphis Pork Ribs. 110
Western Lamb Riblets. 84
Roasted Eggplant Dip. 18
Rosemary Steak. 42
Rosemary-Crusted Leg of Lamb. 96

S
Salmon

Grilled Lobster, Shrimp and
  Calamari Seviche 20
Salmon, Asparagus and Shiitake
  Salad 150
Salmon Salad with Basil Vinaigrette. 144
Tandoori-Style Seafood Kabobs 80
Salmon, Asparagus and Shiitake
  Salad. 150
Salmon Salad with Basil
  Vinaigrette 144
Sausage & Wilted Spinach Salad 154
Serbian Lamb Sausage Kabobs 100

Shellfish

Cajun Grilled Shrimp 66
Grilled Lobster, Shrimp and
  Calamari Seviche 20
Lobster Tails with Tasty Butters. 72
Shrimp Skewers with Tropical
  Fruit Salsa 76
Tandoori-Style Seafood Kabobs 80

Shrimp

Cajun Grilled Shrimp 66
Grilled Lobster, Shrimp and
  Calamari Seviche 20
Shrimp Skewers with Tropical
  Fruit Salsa 76
Tandoori-Style Seafood Kabobs 80
Shrimp Skewers with Tropical
  Fruit Salsa 76

Sides

Grilled Cajun Potato Wedges 10
Herbed Mushroom Vegetable
  Medley 12
Italian Grilled Vegetables. 8
Parmesan Polenta. 22

Index

Sides, (continued)

Portobello Mushrooms Sesame. 14
Zesty Corn-on-the-Cob. 16

Skewered Beef Strips with Spicy
Honey Glaze 38

Skewers

Cajun Grilled Shrimp 66
Chicken Ribbons Satay. 58
Ginger Beef and Carrot Kabobs 24
Grilled Sausage Kabobs with
Apricot Mustard Sauce 114
Lemon-Garlic Shish Kabobs 86
Mediterranean Chicken Kabobs 48
Middle Eastern Kabobs with
Cucumber Sauce. 94
Pork and Plum Kabobs. 104
Serbian Lamb Sausage Kabobs 100
Shrimp Skewers with Tropical
Fruit Salsa 76
Skewered Beef Strips with Spicy
Honey Glaze 38
Tandoori-Style Seafood Kabobs 80
Teriyaki Glazed Beef Kabobs. 28
Turkey Burritos 140
Turkey Teriyaki with Grilled
Mushrooms. 60
Vietnamese Grilled Steak Wraps. 142

Snapper with Pesto Butter. 78
Southwest Chicken 52
Southwest Pesto Burgers 126
Southwestern Lamb Chops with
Charred Corn Relish 102
Spicy Smoked Beef Ribs 32
Sweet and Sour Ham Steaks 120

T

Tandoori-Style Seafood Kabobs. 80
Teriyaki Glazed Beef Kabobs 28
Texas Beef Brisket 30
Thai Barbecued Chicken. 54

Tuna

Grilled Fish Steaks with Tomato
Basil Butter Sauce. 68
Tandoori-Style Seafood Kabobs 80
Tuna Vera Cruz 82

Tuna Vera Cruz 82

Turkey

Jerk Turkey Salad 148
Middle Eastern Kabobs with
Cucumber Sauce. 94
Sausage & Wilted Spinach Salad. 154
Turkey Burritos 140
Turkey Teriyaki with Grilled Mushrooms 60

Turkey Burritos 140
Turkey Teriyaki with Grilled Mushrooms 60

U-V
Vegetarian

Grilled Cajun Potato Wedges 10
Herbed Mushroom Vegetable Medley. 12
Italian Grilled Vegetables. 8
Parmesan Polenta. 22
Portobello Mushrooms Sesame. 14
Roasted Eggplant Dip 18
Zesty Corn-on-the-Cob. 16

Vietnamese Grilled Steak Wraps 142
Vietnamese Loin Steaks with
Black Bean Relish 40

W

Western Lamb Riblets. 84

X-Z

Zesty Corn-on-the-Cob 16

Index

METRIC CONVERSION CHART

VOLUME MEASUREMENTS (dry)

$^1/_8$ teaspoon = 0.5 mL
$^1/_4$ teaspoon = 1 mL
$^1/_2$ teaspoon = 2 mL
$^3/_4$ teaspoon = 4 mL
1 teaspoon = 5 mL
1 tablespoon = 15 mL
2 tablespoons = 30 mL
$^1/_4$ cup = 60 mL
$^1/_3$ cup = 75 mL
$^1/_2$ cup = 125 mL
$^2/_3$ cup = 150 mL
$^3/_4$ cup = 175 mL
1 cup = 250 mL
2 cups = 1 pint = 500 mL
3 cups = 750 mL
4 cups = 1 quart = 1 L

VOLUME MEASUREMENTS (fluid)

1 fluid ounce (2 tablespoons) = 30 mL
4 fluid ounces ($^1/_2$ cup) = 125 mL
8 fluid ounces (1 cup) = 250 mL
12 fluid ounces (1$^1/_2$ cups) = 375 mL
16 fluid ounces (2 cups) = 500 mL

WEIGHTS (mass)

$^1/_2$ ounce = 15 g
1 ounce = 30 g
3 ounces = 90 g
4 ounces = 120 g
8 ounces = 225 g
10 ounces = 285 g
12 ounces = 360 g
16 ounces = 1 pound = 450 g

DIMENSIONS

$^1/_{16}$ inch = 2 mm
$^1/_8$ inch = 3 mm
$^1/_4$ inch = 6 mm
$^1/_2$ inch = 1.5 cm
$^3/_4$ inch = 2 cm
1 inch = 2.5 cm

OVEN TEMPERATURES

250°F = 120°C
275°F = 140°C
300°F = 150°C
325°F = 160°C
350°F = 180°C
375°F = 190°C
400°F = 200°C
425°F = 220°C
450°F = 230°C

BAKING PAN SIZES

Utensil	Size in Inches/Quarts	Metric Volume	Size in Centimeters
Baking or Cake Pan (square or rectangular)	8×8×2	2 L	20×20×5
	9×9×2	2.5 L	23×23×5
	12×8×2	3 L	30×20×5
	13×9×2	3.5 L	33×23×5
Loaf Pan	8×4×3	1.5 L	20×10×7
	9×5×3	2 L	23×13×7
Round Layer Cake Pan	8×1½	1.2 L	20×4
	9×1½	1.5 L	23×4
Pie Plate	8×1¼	750 mL	20×3
	9×1¼	1 L	23×3
Baking Dish or Casserole	1 quart	1 L	—
	1½ quart	1.5 L	—
	2 quart	2 L	—

Metric Chart